THE PURPOSE OF PROSPERITY

by
Frederick K.C. Price, D.D.

Faith One Publishing
Los Angeles, California

Unless otherwise indicated, all Scripture quotations are taken from the *New King James Version* of the Bible. Copyright © 1979, 1980, 1982, Thomas Nelson, Inc., Publishers. Used by permission.

3rd Printing

The Purpose of Prosperity
ISBN 1-883798-55-8
Copyright © 2001 by
Frederick K.C. Price, D.D.
P.O. Box 90000
Los Angeles, CA 90009

Published by Faith One Publishing
7901 South Vermont Avenue
Los Angeles, California 90044

Table of Contents

Introduction

B rave men are never afraid to cut a new path where none has existed before. Once they are convinced of the correctness of their mission, they steel themselves against the onslaught of criticism and march straight toward their goal. So it is with Dr. Frederick K.C. Price. While many preach a gospel of sacrifice and lack, and even take vows of poverty, Dr. Price long ago aligned himself with those who taught that God wants His people to prosper. The Bible supports him: Abraham was merely a friend of God, but God made him "very rich." Joseph had been sold into slavery, but God elevated him to a place where he controlled much of Egypt's great wealth. And Solomon's treasures were legendary, outranking all the other kings of his day.

In our time, the Sultan of Brunei and Microsoft Chairman Bill Gates are applauded for their great stores of riches while ministries practically bankrupt themselves to erect a tiny church or build a little school in Kenya or the Amazon. The critics of prosperity — mainly Christians — would have us believe that God put gold, diamonds, and oil in the earth for His enemies rather than His own blood-bought, blood-washed children. Their criticism of those who preach and teach prosperity, whether intended or not, gives silent assent to the crime lords, drug dealers, and ruthless businesspeople who live in the fine hillside homes and drive the luxurious cars that Christians apparently aren't supposed to have.

Not so, says Dr. Price. The wealth was put here not only for God's people to enjoy, but so He could establish His covenant with them. In fact, God needs His people to prosper if His covenant is to be established in the earth.

Sadly, "Many Christians have misconstrued God's original plan for their prosperity," Dr. Price admits. "When it comes to finances, their thinking has become more selfish and self-centered rather than God-centered. Yes, God wants all of His children to prosper (3 John 2), but there is also a bigger picture to be considered."

God has a purpose for prospering His Church, but it will cost literal billions to accomplish His goal of covering the earth with the gospel. Television, radio, Bibles, books and tapes are some of the more important tools of such a grand outreach plan. Many ministries also send food, clothing, bedding, and medicines. Mission teams must be dispatched to far-off lands and be sustained while they are away. Airline tickets must be bought; work must be done. Corporate America is not going to bankroll this great enterprise; neither will the Mafia. The money has to come from people committed to God's plan. The money has to come from a prosperous Church.

The Editors

1

Why God Wants Us to Prosper

From the very beginning, God's plan for His people was that they grow up spiritually and prosper in every area of living (Genesis 1:26-28). Although His original plans were somewhat thwarted in the Garden with the fall of Adam and Eve, we see His plans for prospering His people being worked out in the lives of Abraham, the father of the Jewish nation, and Abraham's posterity — Isaac and Jacob. Throughout the Old Testament, it appears that God had a twofold objective in causing His people to prosper: One, that those who do not serve Him would see the tangible benefits and blessings that accrue to those who do serve Him. Two, that there be an abundance of *meat* in His storehouse — whether that meat be material or financial — to support the temple/ church and those who took care of the temple/church (the priests/ministers), as well as provide for those who were unable to provide for themselves.

1

Through the years, many Christians have misconstrued God's original plan for their prosperity. When it comes to finances, their thinking has become more selfish and self-centered rather than God-centered. Yes, God wants all of His children to prosper (3 John 2), but there is also a bigger picture to be considered.

We are living in a world that is basically hell-bound. When we hear that three-fourths of the world's population has never heard the gospel, and we see the moral decay and confusion that have taken place in the Church in recent years, we — the body of Christ — have far to go in understanding God's original purpose for prospering His children.

It is my aim to explore in depth what is the real purpose for God's prosperity, how to achieve it, and what we are to do with it once we get it. For the believer whose aim is to live a godly life, the heavenly Father is always available to work on his or her behalf. The Bible tells us that it is through His faithful children that God has, does, and will reach out to a lost and dying world. In other words, we are all that God has through which to do His mighty works in the earth. I have asked myself this question, and now I ask you: *If we are all that God has, is God in trouble?*

I want to begin this important study on the purpose of prosperity with a very familiar scripture that believers hear all the time but few understand its implication:

Deuteronomy 8:18:

"And you shall remember the Lord your God, for it is He who gives you power to get wealth,

that He may establish His covenant which He swore to your fathers, as it is this day."

This awesome statement was made to the children of Israel on their way to the Promised Land. The Israelites had been in Egyptian bondage for more than 430 years. They had cried out to Jehovah God for deliverance, and He sent them the Prophet Moses as their deliverer. God had promised them that He would give them a land flowing with milk and honey. With Moses leading the way, the Israelites left Egypt and crossed the Red Sea. God showed great signs and wonders on their behalf. They traversed the wilderness, and stood on the banks of the Jordan River. Through Moses, God spoke to the people and made that awesome promise.

...for it is He who gives you power....

The word *power* in this verse literally means "authority, right or privilege." Obviously, if God wants to give someone the right or privilege to get wealth, He cannot be against His children having wealth. To understand this covenant of wealth that is talked about in Deuteronomy 8:18, it would be profitable for us to explore the heart of God as recorded in the Bible.

Matthew 6:33:

"But seek first the kingdom of God and His righteousness, and all these things shall be added to you."

In exploring the heart of God, we need to ask ourselves some questions: *What is the kingdom of God? What is God's covenant? What is closest to the heart of God? When Jesus walked the earth what was closest to His heart?* Jesus said in John 5:30 that He came not to do His own will but the will of the Father who sent Him. In John 6:38 - 40 He stated it this way:

> **38** **"For I have come down from heaven, not to do My own will, but the will of Him who sent Me.**
>
> **39** **"This is the will of the Father who sent Me, that of all that He has given Me I should lose nothing, but should raise it up at the last day.**
>
> **40** **"And this is the will of Him who sent Me, that everyone who sees the Son and believes in Him may have everlasting life; and I will raise him up at the last day."**

According to this scripture, God's will is that everyone come into a knowledge of His Son Jesus Christ and receive Him so they can be saved. That way the relationship that God had with man before the fall of Adam can be re-established.

Let's look at another passage of scripture to see the heart of the Father with regard to man's salvation:

Luke 19:1-10:

> **1** **Then Jesus entered and passed through Jericho.**
>
> **2** **Now behold, there was a man named Zacchaeus who was a chief tax collector, and he was rich.**

3   **And he sought to see who Jesus was, but could not because of the crowd, for he was of short stature.**

4   **So he ran ahead and climbed up into a sycamore tree to see Him, for He was going to pass that way.**

5   **And when Jesus came to the place, He looked up and saw him, and said to him, "Zacchaeus, make haste and come down, for today I must stay at your house."**

6   **So He made haste and came down, and received Him joyfully.**

7   **But when they saw it, they all complained, saying, "He has gone to be a guest with a man who is a sinner."**

8   **Then Zacchaeus stood and said to the Lord, "Look, Lord, I give half of my goods to the poor; and if I have taken anything from anyone by false accusation, I restore fourfold."**

9   **And Jesus said to him, "Today salvation has come to this house, because he also is a son of Abraham;**

10   **"for the Son of Man has come to seek and to save that which was lost."**

There is the will of God stated in a nutshell: **to seek and to save that which was lost.** Obviously, it must take wealth to seek and to save the lost, and that is why God wants us to have wealth.

We as Christians are God's instruments on earth. Jesus is no longer here physically. The Holy Spirit is the only Person of the Godhead who is present in the earth realm today, and He only works through yielded vessels in the body of Christ. We are all that God has, and He is depending on us to do the work on earth in seeking and saving the lost.

When Jesus was ready to go back to heaven, He said to His disciples, and ultimately down through time to all of us who would come into the body of Christ and become His disciples, **"Go into all the world and preach the gospel to every creature"** (Mark 16:15). Notice He didn't say, "Build the church and wait for the world to come to you." No, He said for us to go into the world and seek and save the lost.

I'm going to say something that some folk might find shocking, but it is nonetheless true: The local church is not for the purpose of getting people saved. The local church is for the purpose of shepherding the "sheep" and "lambs" to grow them up so they can go out and seek and save the lost. The local church is to feed the sheep and lambs spiritual food so they can get fat on the Word and, in turn, go out and seek and save more of the lost. And this is to go on and on until Jesus returns. That is the way it is supposed to work.

But what has happened is that a lot of Christians have made prosperity a thing for me, myself, and I — us three. They have made the prosperity message a way to get bigger houses, newer cars, more designer clothes, and a nice bank account. Many have forgotten about those in the world who don't know Jesus, and are lost and on their way to hell.

A Godly Point of Satisfaction

Where is your godly point of satisfaction? In other words, if you happen to be caught up in a cycle of accruing bigger and bigger, when are you going to get enough material things so that it is not all about you spending all of your finances on your wants and desires, and not be able to financially support the spreading of the gospel?

I am not knocking any of those things I mentioned. God is not opposed to those things, because we read in Matthew 6:33 to **seek first the kingdom**. He did not say, "to seek *only.*" I believe that in the pursuit of wealth, the Church has lost sight of its priorities and has put seeking the lost on the back burner. I asked this question before, but because it is so important, I want to ask it again: *If we are all that God has to seek and save the lost, is God in trouble?* He does not have any angels to preach the gospel or send on errands of mercy. He only has us. If we do not preach the gospel, who is going to do it? The wealth is for the body of Christ to have the funds to go into all the world and preach the gospel, and that is why God wants us to prosper.

It is amazing to me, but most Christians are committed to giving just so much money. Yet, it is God who gives us the wisdom and the ability to do our jobs. We have to do better. We cross paths on a daily basis with multitudes of people who are dying and going to hell, and we hold in our hands the keys to the Kingdom; yet, many of us don't even open our mouths to witness to them.

Sometimes you need to satisfy a man's natural physical hunger before you tell him about the Kingdom. He may be so hungry physically that he cannot hear what is being said. So you may have to spend a little time with him and feed the man before he is in a position to listen to what you have to say about the things of God. To feed him and many like him costs money. Where is that money going to come from? That is why we need the wealth.

Luke 10:25-37:

25 And behold, a certain lawyer stood up and tested Him, saying, "Teacher, what shall I do to inherit eternal life?"

26 He said to him, "What is written in the law? What is your reading of it?"

27 So he answered and said, "'*You shall love the Lord your God with all your heart, with all your soul, with all your strength, and with all your mind,' and 'your neighbor as yourself.'"* [If you love God with all your heart, all your soul, all your strength, and all your mind, you will love Him with all your money, too.]

28 And He said to him, "You have answered rightly; do this and you will live."

29 But he, wanting to justify himself, said to Jesus, "And who is my neighbor?"

30 Then Jesus answered and said: "A certain man went down from Jerusalem to Jericho, and fell among

thieves, who stripped him of his clothing, wounded him, and departed, leaving him half dead.

31 "Now by chance a certain priest came down that road. And when he saw him, he passed by on the other side.

32 "Likewise a Levite, when he arrived at the place, came and looked, and passed by on the other side.

33 "But a certain Samaritan, as he journeyed, came where he was. And when he saw him, he had compassion.

34 "So he went to him and bandaged his wounds, pouring on oil and wine; and he set him on his own animal, brought him to an inn, and took care of him.

35 "On the next day, when he departed, he took out two denarii, gave them to the innkeeper, and said to him, 'Take care of him; and whatever more you spend, when I come again, I will repay you.'

36 "So which of these three do you think was neighbor to him who fell among the thieves?"

37 And he said, "He who showed mercy on him." Then Jesus said to him, "Go and do likewise."

The thieves' philosophy was, "What is yours is mine, and I'm taking it." They left the poor man half dead. The philosophy of the priest and the Levite who saw this man lying at the roadside was, "What is mine is mine, and I don't intend to share it with anyone." They forgot all about Deuteronomy 8:18 and that it was God who gave them the power to get the wealth in the first place.

But notice the compassion of the Samaritan! He saw someone in need and went to his aid. What a man! What a heart! The Samaritan's philosophy was, "What is mine is thine, and if you need it, here it is." Is your philosophy that of the priest? The Levite? Or the Samaritan? God wants His children to be like the Samaritan and care about those who are lost, suffering, and in need of the compassion of Jesus.

God is all about redemption. But it is going to take a lot of money to get the job done. For example, on some television stations it costs more than $30,000 an hour to broadcast our *Ever Increasing Faith* program. Television and radio are tremendous tools we can use to reach the lost around the world, but it costs a great deal of money to buy airtime. It costs a lot of money to print Bibles, and Christian books and tapes. Everything costs megabucks, and the money for God's projects has to come from God's people. That places you and me in a position of being stewards. And guess what? Judgment Day is coming, and one day at the heavenly audit, we are going to have to give an account of how faithful we have been with what has been entrusted to our care for the proclamation of the gospel.

The beautiful thing is that in the process of gaining wealth so that we can be workers together with God in seeking the lost, all our own needs and desires (that are consistent with a godly life) are met in the process. It is not an either/or thing; it is both. In other words, we can have it all. But there are biblical principles that must be put into operation if the wealth is to come to us.

Jesus said He came "to seek and to save the lost," but Satan, the archenemy of God, comes to seek and to destroy. Jesus said in John 10:10: **"The thief does not come except to steal, and to kill, and to destroy."** So, we can expect to have satanic opposition to keep us from getting the wealth. Satan knows that if we get the wealth to seek the lost, then he will be out of business, so he will do everything he can to stop us from getting the wealth.

Overcoming the Enemy

The devil's plan is to keep you struggling from daylight until dark. That way, your life becomes simply the pursuit of trying to make ends meet and you never get your priorities in line with God's plan to seek and save the lost. You have to get past that. You have to become financially independent of the circumstances so that you make the rules of how you spend your money instead of the devil and society making the rules for you. Think about it. I don't care how beautiful the day looks. In all likelihood, you cannot simply get your gear and go fishing with the boys. You have to punch that clock because if you do not, you will not get a paycheck, and if you do not get a paycheck, you are going to be up a creek in a boat with no oars. But there is a place in God where you can become financially independent; you just have to learn where that place is, remembering the whole time that the purpose for your becoming financially independent is not for you to squander it all on you so that you can change cars every thirty days, or buy more clothes or go on expensive vacations, but rather it is to seek and to save that which was lost.

Before we can be successful in our pursuit of prosperity, we need to determine from the Word that it is God's will for us to prosper. If you do not know it is the will of God for you personally to prosper, you may not be able to exercise faith to believe to be prosperous and financially independent. Faith can only be exercised where the will of God is known. For example, if you do not know that it is God's will for you to be well or healed, you cannot exercise faith to believe to be healed, because faith is based only upon the revealed will of God, and God's will is revealed in the Bible.

In seeking the lost, we have two options: We can be *goers* or we can be *senders.* Those who are out there seeking the lost need to be financially supported. Everyone cannot simply pick up and go out on the mission field; some people do have that call and will go, but someone has to support them so these *goers* can spend all their time ministering to the needs of people and seeking the lost. It takes wealth to *send* or to *go.* Therefore, we have to know that God wants us to prosper so that we will be able to receive His blessings that will put us in the position of being a *sender* or even a *goer.*

The thing about it, there is no shortage of wealth. It is just in the wrong hands. It has to get into the hands of people who understand that seeking the Kingdom is first. It has to get into the hands of people who have a mind to do the will of God. Satan has very cleverly siphoned off the wealth of the world, and put it into the hands of people who do not care about the things of God. We, the body of Christ, have to determine that we are going to get a big piece of the pie so we can give into the Kingdom for the spreading of the gospel.

Prerequisites for Prospering

Joshua 1:8:

"This Book of the Law shall not depart from your mouth, but you shall meditate in it day and night, that you may observe to do according to all that is written in it. For then you will make your way prosperous, and then you will have good success."

The *Book of the Law* means the Word of God. All of the revelation God has given to man is called progressive revelation. Actually, our education system works the same way. For example, educators do not give a child preschool, grammar school, middle school, high school, college, and graduate school all in one week. They have made education progressive and in keeping with a student's chronological age and mental aptitude so that the student will receive, assimilate, digest, and regurgitate, as it were, all the learning that goes with education at a pace that is realistic. All of God's Word is His Law. The Bible — both the Old and New Testament — is God's Word, and He does not make suggestions in it. What He says in the Bible is always His command.

13

Here is the progression God outlines in this verse:

Shall not depart from your mouth means that the Word of God should not *stop* going out of your mouth. In other words, you should always be about speaking the Word of God.

But you shall meditate in it day and night does not mean the traditional concept of meditation. In the original Hebrew language, *meditate* means "to mutter" or "to mumble." It also means to speak very softly, just loud enough for you to hear yourself speak.

Day and night does not mean all day twelve hours and all night twelve hours. If this were the case, you would not be able to do anything else. This terminology simply means to do something daily — not just on Sundays.

That you may observe to do.... A lot of people observe, but they do not do what they observe. I would wager that if you have been a Christian or even been around Christians for any length of time, you or the Christians you know have not actually been out there seeking and saving that which was lost, even though you probably have read this scripture many times in the Bible. We can see that Christians are not following this scripture, because if they were, the world would not be in such a sad condition.

Now we come to what this scripture is all about. That is, if we follow the first three requisites:

For then you will make your way prosperous.... Notice, God will not make your way prosperous. YOU WILL. Your degree of prosperity is your responsibility. So, if you do not like what you have been receiving in life, go look in the mirror. You are the problem — not the circumstances, not God, not the devil, but *you.*

14

Personally, I like it that God has put the prosperity ball in my court, because it puts me on par with everyone else. I have neither an advantage nor a disadvantage. All I have to do is be obedient to the Word. God is bigger than all the ethnic groups of the world combined, so no one group can hold me down. He is the Creator of the universe, so if He tells me I can do something, then I take Him at His Word and I go for it.

I have proven that God's Word works in my own personal life, but God wants to bring forth the promises in His Word for every one of His blood-bought children. To manifest those promises in your life, however, you are going to have to pay your dues. I have paid my dues. I took time to study the Bible, confess the Word, be a giver, and do all the other things the Word told me to do with regard to living a moral life. That is why I am prospering today. The good news is He will do the same for you.

And then you will have good success. This almost seems a play on words, because in our society the word *success* connotes the idea of a winner. You do not think of the word *defeat* when you hear the word *success*. But if that's so, why does it say "good success"? I believe God put it this way to alert us to the fact that there is such a thing as "bad success."

If you had 27 million dollars in the bank, owned five houses free and clear, had several automobiles parked in your garage, owned a jet airplane, and a yacht, the world would certainly classify you as being successful. But while you have all those things, your wife is making out with the gardener, the dog raped the cat and the canary swallowed the goldfish. You don't know who your friends are because you do not know

15

whether they like you or like what your money can buy for them. You cannot trust anyone. You are so worried and stressed out that your stomach is torn up with ulcers, and you cannot eat anything. The world might classify you as being successful, yet you are miserable. That is "bad success."

"Good success" is when you have all of the aforementioned commodities, but the gardener is not in the deal, and all is great between you and your wife. All your kids are saved and filled with the Holy Spirit. You have a multitude of friends who love you and are not out for what they can get, and you are walking in divine health. That is good success.

God's People Have Been Misinformed

We are establishing the fact that God wants us to prosper, because down through the ages, people have been given wrong information that says it is ungodly to be materially prosperous. Some people even call it worldly to be prosperous, which is so stupid because everything here is in the world.

Psalm 1:1-3:

1   **Blessed is the man who walks not in the counsel of the ungodly** [number one], **nor stands in the path of sinners** [number two], **nor sits in the seat of the scornful** [number three];

2   **But his delight is in the law of the Lord,** [There is that law of the Lord again, number 4] **and in His law he**

meditates day and night. [There is that day and night again. Notice that Verse 3 is predicated on verses 1 and 2.]

3   **He shall be like a tree planted by the rivers of water, that brings forth its fruit in its season, whose leaf also shall not wither; and whatever he does shall prosper.**

This passage tells us that God absolutely wants His children to prosper. Notice again that there are some prerequisites, which are stated in verses 1 and 2. The blessings do not work automatically. As I said before, if you are not prospering, then you need to check yourself out and determine what the problem is.

If we are duped into thinking that Christians are not supposed to prosper or that prosperity is materialistic, then we may not even be alert to the opportunities God can make available to us to prosper. The Bible says in the mouth of two or three witnesses let every word be established (2 Corinthians 13:1). I gave you Joshua 1 and Psalm 1 as witnesses, but I want to go beyond these two.

Psalm 35:27:

Let them shout for joy and be glad, who favor my righteous cause; and let them say continually, "Let the Lord be magnified, who has pleasure in the prosperity of His servant."

17

If God has pleasure in the prosperity of His servant, He certainly would have displeasure in the poverty of His own blood-bought child. Someone once said to me, "Well, if that is true pastor, why does God allow poverty?" God allows poverty because we allow it. It is up to us to do something about poverty. It is not His will that you be poor or sick, but He has designed the system in order to put the choice of being poor or sick into our own hands. If we choose to be poor or sick, He has no choice but to allow it.

Under the Old Covenant, the children of Israel, the nation through which God would bring His Word, and ultimately His redemption of mankind, were not classified as God's children, but His servants. No one could be called a child of God until he or she had accepted Jesus Christ as Savior, and Jesus had not come yet. The Israelites were the children of Israel and were classified as servants of Jehovah. But under the New Covenant, when a person receives Christ as Savior and Lord, then he or she is classified as a child of God.

There is a crazy idea being fostered in the world today called the "fatherhood of God and the brotherhood of man." That idea is erroneous and unscriptural. You cannot be my brother unless we have the same father. Yes, everybody is a creation of God, but so are the rocks and mountains. Just because God created something does not make it His child, and unless you have accepted Jesus Christ as Savior, you are not in a position to respond as a child of God. Let me show you what I am talking about.

John 1:6-13:

6   **There was a man sent from God, whose name was John.**

7   **This man came for a witness, to bear witness of the Light, that all through him might believe.**

8   **He was not that Light, but was sent to bear witness of that Light.**

9   **That was the true Light which gives light to every man coming into the world.**

10   **He was in the world, and the world was made through Him, and the world did not know Him.**

11   **He came to His own** [meaning Israel], **and His own did not receive Him.**

12   **But as many as received Him, to them He gave the right to become children of God, to those who believe in His name:**

13   **who were born, not of blood, nor of the will of the flesh, nor of the will of man, but of God.**

Notice the latter part of that twelfth verse:

...to them He gave the right to become children of God...

If God has to give the right to someone to become a child of His, that person must not have already been His child.

A person is not a child of God unless he or she receives Jesus as Savior and Lord. So, there is no such thing as the fatherhood of God and the brotherhood of man.

God Wants His Children to Prosper

We need to get the idea firmly established in our hearts that God wants all His children to prosper, so we can do what we need to do to get wealth to finance the Kingdom.

Job 36:5-11:

5 **Behold, God is mighty, but despises no one; He is mighty in strength of understanding.**

6 **He does not preserve the life of the wicked, but gives justice to the oppressed.**

7 **He does not withdraw His eyes from the righteous; but they are on the throne with kings, for He has seated them forever, and they are exalted.**

8 **And if they are bound in fetters, held in the cords of affliction,**

9 **Then He tells them their work and their transgressions — that they have acted defiantly.**

10 **He also opens their ear to instruction, and commands that they turn from iniquity.**

11   **If they obey and serve Him, they**
      shall spend their days in prosperity,
      and their years in pleasures.

Theses verses inform us that God is not opposed to me or you prospering. But again, notice the prerequisites. We have to live a godly life in order to spend our days in prosperity. Now let's move over into the New Testament:

3 John 2:

Beloved, I pray that you may prosper in all things and be in health, just as your soul prospers.

Here, the Apostle John is talking to the children of God, and not just to people who belong to a church. Many people go to church, have even been baptized and received into membership, but they still may not be saved. A whole lot of folk have been confirmed, refirmed, unfirmed, but they have never accepted Jesus. They may have accepted a particular denomination, but that does not make them a Christian. *"Well, Pastor, I was baptized when I was a child, and confirmed when I was seven."* Yes, and you are on your way to hell, too, and not because you are a bad person.

People have it all mixed up. They think that doing bad things is what makes them a sinner. No, it is the way they were born that makes them a sinner. All of us started out born in sin and conceived in iniquity (Psalm 51:5-6); that is why we need to become children of God, and the only way to do that is to receive Jesus Christ.

The Purpose of Prosperity

I believe that we have clearly established from the Word that God wants us to prosper so that we can be workers together with Him in proclaiming the gospel.

2

We Are God's Pipeline

Satan has used the notion that Jesus and the apostles were poor to keep Christians from pursuing wealth, or even thinking about the possibility of being prosperous. Many people have that idea and think, "Well, if Jesus did not have anything, then the body of Christ shouldn't."

If you have that kind of mindset, then you will not be open to become a channel through which God can pipe wealth so that the lost can be sought and won. I want to be a pipeline for God; that is why I am believing to be wealthy and to have millions of dollars. I do not need millions of dollars for me, but I want to be able to plant seed into the Kingdom of God.

It was not too long ago that someone gave $10 million to a university as an endowment. Think of what the Church could do with that much money; think of how many hungry people we could feed with that amount of money; think of how many *goers* we could support on the foreign field if we had $10 million.

As I said, Satan uses this ploy of getting Christians to think, "Well, you know, Brother Price, it's nice to say we should be prosperous and wealthy and should have material things. But you know it's difficult for me to accept that concept in total because, as I remember, Jesus and the apostles were not people of means. Jesus did not own a house or any property or cattle. In fact, He didn't seem to have anything, so I have a difficult time subscribing to the concept that I should have, when I look at my Lord Jesus."

You have to get past these roadblocks so they will not cause you to have a sense of guilt if you prosper materially. I want to show you that the poverty mentality is not in line with what the Bible says.

Matthew 8:18-20:

> **18** **And when Jesus saw great multitudes about Him, He gave a command to depart to the other side.**
>
> **19** **Then a certain scribe came and said to Him, "Teacher, I will follow You wherever You go."**
>
> **20** **And Jesus said to him, "Foxes have holes and birds of the air have nests, but the Son of Man has nowhere to lay His head."**

I grant you it does sound like Jesus did not have much, but let's explore a little bit more to see what Jesus meant when He said He had "nowhere to lay His head."

24

Mark 4:35-38:

35   On the same day, when evening had
come, He [Jesus] said to them, "Let
us cross over to the other side."

36   Now when they had left the multitude,
they took Him along in the boat as
He was. And other little boats were
also with Him.

37   And a great windstorm arose, and the
waves beat into the boat, so that it
was already filling.

38   But He was in the stern, asleep on a
pillow....

All the writer had to say was that "He was asleep," and
we would have known that Jesus was not awake. Why tell us
that He had His head on a pillow? I believe the Holy Spirit put
it this way so as to defuse the idea that we read in Matthew
about Jesus not having any place to lay His head. He had His
head on a pillow, so He did have some place to lay His head. I
want to re-examine Matthew 8 in light of this.

The scribe came to Jesus and said that he would follow Him wherever He went. Jesus responded by saying that
foxes have holes and birds have nests, but He had nowhere
to lay His head. What Jesus actually meant was that nor-
mally where a person lays his head is his place of abode.
That was why He used the examples of foxes and birds,
because their holes and nests were their dwelling places. He

25

did not have a permanent dwelling place because He was to be here on earth for a limited time. He was not going to have a wife or children, or buy property, or own a home, because He was on an itinerant assignment in ministry to the nation of Israel, and if the young man wanted to follow Jesus, he would have to understand there would be no permanent residence for him.

There was a time in my spiritual walk, before I found out about faith, when I thought Christians were not supposed to have anything. In fact, I thought it was a mark of worldliness to have material things. I felt we were supposed to have just enough to exist on, because after all, we were going to have it all over there on the other side, in the sweet bye-and-bye. Even if God had found some way to pipe prosperity to me, I would not have been open to receive it until I learned to walk by faith and not by sight. Jesus went back to heaven and told us to finish the work He started. He said the Church would do greater works than He did. That means we should reach more people because there are more of us, and that is why He has given the body of Christ the power to get the wealth in order to do it.

Let's look at another passage of scripture that shows that God's will is for His children to prosper.

1 Timothy 6:17:

Command those who are rich in this present age not to be haughty, nor to trust in uncertain riches but in the living God, who gives us richly all things to enjoy.

26

For years, when I read this scripture, I thought that Paul was referring to rich sinners. Christians were not supposed to be rich. I assumed He was saying: *"Command those folks that are rich out there; don't let them get high minded with their wealth and that kind of thing. "* But let's use our heads for a moment. How many Christians personally know rich sinners to such an extent that they could advise them about what they should do with their wealth? Very, very few. If that is the case, then Paul had to be talking about rich Christians.

What Paul was telling these Christians was not to get the big head because they had money, and not to trust in those riches. He was telling them, in essence, to put their total trust in God who gives us richly all things to enjoy. Notice what is conspicuous in its absence: Paul did not command Timothy to tell the rich to get rid of their riches. This concept has been fostered throughout Christianity for years: *If you come to Christ, you are supposed to give up everything and be broke.* That concept has probably scared off many rich people from coming into the Kingdom. When it comes to "giving up everything," there are two ways to do this: One way is to give everything away, and the other way is to commit everything to the Lord. *Lord, what would You have me to do? I am a steward of what You have entrusted to me. What is Your will?* That is what God wants us to do. He does not want us to give away everything, because He is the One who gives it to us in the first place, but He does it for a purpose.

Christianity was brand-new when the apostles first went out and began to proclaim the gospel, and the people began to believe their teaching. When these new converts accepted Jesus, many of them were already wealthy. God did not want them to get rid of their wealth, once they became saved. He wanted them to dedicate their wealth to Him for the spreading of the gospel.

It is amazing how many people will put their money into the hands of a financial analyst they don't even know based solely on someone's recommendation or some advertisement they see on television. But yet they are afraid to turn their money over to God, and He is the One to whom they should have absolutely no fear of turning over their money. Do you know why? We do not have to be concerned about God embezzling our funds. We don't have to be concerned about Him taking advantage of us, because He has so much more than we will ever have in a million lifetimes. God does not need our money; whatever money we give Him, it is always for the benefit of the body of Christ or lost humanity.

Who gives us richly all things to enjoy. It is interesting that Paul uses the word richly. The actual Greek word used in this text means lavishly, and lavish means "copiously and abundantly supplied." Unfortunately, even today, there are a number of Christians who believe that we are not supposed to enjoy life. But the Bible says, God gives us lavishly all things to enjoy.

Some Christians did not have anything when they first came into the knowledge of faith and were having a lot of problems. Through Bible teaching, they have learned how to believe God and have received many material blessings. But many still have a lot of financial problems, because if they didn't, they would be giving more into the Kingdom than they do. They are still bound. They have a bigger house and bigger cars, but they have bigger payments, too. They are still using up all of their resources and are not making the Kingdom a priority in their lives. The Lord has told us that it is He who gives us the ability to get wealth to establish His covenant — not our agendas, but His covenant. Paul said in Philippians 2:5: **Let this mind be in you which was also in Christ Jesus.** Notice, it says let, which means we control what we let into our minds.

If Christ is in us, and the scriptures say He is, then His mindset ought to be in us, and Jesus' mindset is seeking and saving the lost. Our attitude should be, "Lord, what would you have me to do with what you have given me?" Instead, we are telling God what we are going to do with what He has given us: "This prosperity, Lord, is going to get me a new car. Now if by chance there are some crumbs left over, I might, dedicate some of them to seeking and saving the lost." That is the attitude of many Christians today, and it is a wrong attitude.

I Timothy 6:18:

Let them do good, that they be rich in good works, ready to give, willing to share.

To seek and to save that which is lost is to do good. Acts 10:38 says: **"how God anointed Jesus of Nazareth with the Holy Spirit and with power, who went about doing good and healing all who were oppressed by the devil...."** If we let His mind be in us, then we will be about doing good. And you can do a whole lot more good with wealth than you can with a welfare check.

Do you think when Jesus fed the multitudes He was just in the business of having an outdoor open-air restaurant? No, He knew that if you get a man's stomach full, he is in a better position to listen to what you have to say. Jesus was smart enough to know that if He had a satisfied, captive audience, He could give them the Word. He fed five thousand men, plus women and children, and you know you will always have twice as many women and children, so He probably fed about 15 thousand people. How did He get the people's attention? He didn't say, "I came to feed." He said, "I came to seek and save." Jesus understood that it would take feeding the people to get them into a position to hear what He had to say, just as it may take us feeding the people to get them into a position to be saved. That is why we need the wealth piped to us.

At Crenshaw Christian Center, we have what we call a Community Outreach Program. At one time this program cost us more than $20 thousand a week in addition to our other expenses and services we were providing to our parishioners. The program, which provides food and clothing to people in need, cost us more than $80 thousand a month, and about $1 million a year. But look at the potential for seeking the lost! Jesus said for us to **be wise as serpents and harmless as doves** (Matthew 10:16), which means we have to use the wisdom God gives us to develop creative ideas to reach the lost. Before we give the people food and clothing, we give them spiritual food — the Word of God.

Your brain, your abilities, and your talents are not just yours. These are gifts that have been planted in you by God. The Lord gives abilities and talents to people. He has to.

Otherwise, why would somebody want to be a doctor or a nurse? They surely can make more money and not work as hard as they do — always on call, never really a free moment. Why would anyone want to be a policeman? There you are trying to help folk, and they end up calling you a pig. Thank God for firemen who are willing to go out on some hillside with a bunch of weeds and grass to fight a fire and inhale all that deadly smoke to keep our houses from burning down. Thank God for the gardeners, cooks, trash people, and businesspeople that help us live better lives every day. The point I want to make is that it is God who puts all these abilities in us, and entrusts them to our care, ultimately for the purpose of seeking and saving that which was lost.

...that they be rich in good works, ready to give, willing to share.

Are you ready to give, willing to share? If you are not a tither, you are not willing to give or to share. *"I don't believe in tithing, Brother Price."* Then you don't believe in God. You may think you do, but you don't. Look at your right hand; do you know that God is depending upon that hand to get His works done on earth? He is depending on you to lay that hand on the sick. Look down at your feet? Do you know God is depending upon those feet to go on errands of mercy and to take the gospel to the lost? Look in the mirror at your mouth. Do you know that God is depending upon that mouth to speak to the world about Jesus and what He has provided for all mankind — at least for those who are willing to receive Him as Savior? We are all that God has.

If you are not open to the prospect of prospering, then God cannot funnel or pipe the resources to you. If there were no body of Christ in the earth realm, who would God give the power to get wealth to? We are His children, so He has to give it to us, but He doesn't just pour it out on us. We know this because if that were true, every Christian would be a multimillionaire right now. But it does not work that way.

It is easy to say you are willing to share when you do not have anything to share, but can God trust you with His wealth? The Bible principle is that **"He who is faithful in what is least is faithful also in much"** (Luke 16:10). Faithfulness is a character trait or quality that you have irrespective of what amount you have the opportunity to oversee. A faithful person will be as faithful with one dollar as he would be with a million dollars.

Some people cannot get to church on time to save their lives. In fact, some people act as if it would be against their belief if they were to be in church and in their seats when the service starts. They lack faithfulness. How can God trust you with wealth, if you cannot even make it to church on time to serve Him? Our Sunday service begins promptly at 9:30 a.m., but some people think nothing of strolling in at 9:45 or even 10:00 every Sunday. It is amazing. But these same parishioners would be the first to say how desperately they need a financial blessing. How can God bless them when they do not give Him the honor He deserves by being on time for the service? And yet they almost break the speed limit getting to work on time. This sounds like a little thing, but if you can't be trusted with a little thing like getting to church on time, how can you be trusted with a big thing like a lot of money being piped to you?

This may all sound disconnected, but it is not. We have to prove ourselves faithful if we are going to be workers together with the Lord in getting the job done. He wants to get people saved, so Jesus can return, and we can get on with the real business of living.

Were Jesus and the Apostles Poor?

The churches that I attended before establishing Crenshaw Christian Center left me with the idea that Jesus and the apostles were not men of means; they were very spiritually oriented, but very poor. Many portraits today show Jesus with a halo around His head, and standing about two inches off the ground. This is the concept that most of the Christian world has of Jesus: They believe that He was so heavenly minded, that He was detached from earthly things, and He and His apostles never had anything from a material point of view. Jesus was not poor, neither were the apostles. In fact, the Word implies that Jesus and the apostles were actually financially well off. If you come to the Bible with traditionally tinted glasses of denominationalism and theological concepts, you will read right over what the Word says.

Mark 1:16:

And as He walked by the Sea of Galilee, He saw Simon and Andrew his brother casting a net into the sea; for they were fishermen.

Anyone can fish, but everyone who fishes is not a fisherman. I read it for years and missed it. I thought I was reading, "They were fishing," and never stopped to analyze the fact that they were fishermen; fishing was their profession.

Mark 1:17-18:

> **17** **Then Jesus said to them, "Follow Me, and I will make you become fishers of men."**
>
> **18** **They immediately left their nets and followed Him.**

You have to understand this about the Bible: It is not a history book about man on earth. If you read from Genesis to Revelation, there is much concerning man on the earth that has been left out. The Bible does not tell us anything about world leaders or world history or the dinosaurs, or anything like that. The Bible is a history of God dealing spiritual with mankind. So the only thing we are going to find in the Bible, basically, is what concerns man from a redemptive point of view. For example, how many times do you find it recorded that Jesus and the apostles could not go on a teaching mission because it was raining? It never mentions anything about rain in this context because it doesn't have to do with the plan of redemption. There are many things that happened that the Bible does not even mention, and it takes spiritual perception to understand what is being said.

Verse 18 tells us that Peter and Andrew immediately left their boat and followed Jesus. To us that does not make sense. Because our first thought would be: "What about their families?" The second thought would be: "How can they leave a business immediately?" Obviously, between Verse 17, when Jesus saw them, and their leaving immediately, something went on, but the Bible does not tell us per se because it does not have anything to do with man's redemption.

These men were fishermen; that means they were businessmen. Businesspeople do not just walk away from their businesses unless they know what they are walking toward. No one can just walk up to you and tell you to leave your job without talking about some kind of compensation. For example, these men would want to know at least what kind of benefits Jesus was offering. You don't just walk off a job unless you are dumb and stupid like I was at one time in my life. I walked off a good job because I was immature, and I paid for it later. I suffered and my family suffered, and my behind got kicked for years as a result of that bad move. These men could not afford to just go off with Jesus unless they, at the least, made a lateral move.

Mark 1:19-20:

> **19** **When He had gone a little farther from there, He saw James the son of Zebedee, and John his brother, who also were in the boat mending their nets.**

> **20** **And immediately He called them, and they left their father Zebedee in the boat with the hired servants, and went after Him.**

Poor folk do not have hired servants. If you hire someone to work for you, you have to have enough income to pay that employee and all of your expenses for the operation of the business, and then make a profit. Notice it says, **they left their father Zebedee in the boat with the hired servants** — hired servants, plural, which means they had more than one. These men were not just poor people sitting by the welfare office with nothing to do when Jesus called them. He had to make them a lucrative offer, or they would not have been good businessmen to just pack up and go. Jesus did not hypnotize them; He did not throw a spiritual cape over their heads and drag them off screaming and hollering. They were businessmen with hired servants working for them. They could not just get up and leave without finding out: "What is in this for me? How are we going to work this deal? Right now, I call my own shots. What kind of time will I have to put in if I come and work for you?" These men were the only ones Jesus could afford to call to go with Him. He could not call illiterate, unemployed people to help spread the gospel.

I said that Jesus had plenty materially. He was not the poor lowly Son of God that we have traditionally thought Him to be.

John 13:18-29:

18　"I do not speak concerning all of you. I know whom I have chosen; but that the Scripture may be fulfilled, *'He who eats bread with Me has lifted up his heel against Me.'*

19　"Now I tell you before it comes, that when it does come to pass, you may believe that I am *He.*

20   "Most assuredly, I say to you, he who receives whomever I send receives Me; and he who receives Me receives Him who sent Me."

21   When Jesus had said these things, He was troubled in spirit, and testified and said, "Most assuredly, I say to you, one of you will betray Me."

22   Then the disciples looked at one another, perplexed about whom He spoke.

23   Now there was leaning on Jesus' bosom one of His disciples, whom Jesus loved.

24   Simon Peter therefore motioned to him to ask who it was of whom He spoke.

25   Then, leaning back on Jesus' breast, he said to Him, "Lord, who is it?"

26   Jesus answered, "It is he to whom I shall give a piece of bread when I have dipped it." And having dipped the bread, He gave it to Judas Iscariot, *the son* of Simon.

27   Now after the piece of bread, Satan entered him. Then Jesus said to him, "What you do, do quickly."

28   **But no one at the table knew for what reason He said this to him.**

29   **For some thought, because Judas had the money box....**

Now I want to deal with this money box.
Let's go over to John 12:3-6:

3   **Then Mary took a pound of very costly oil of spikenard, anointed the feet of Jesus, and wiped His feet with her hair. And the house was filled with the fragrance of the oil.**

4   **But one of His disciples, Judas Iscariot, Simon's son, who would betray Him, said,**

5   **"Why was this fragrant oil not sold for three hundred denarii and given to the poor?"**

6   **This he said, not that he cared for the poor, but because he was a thief, and had the money box; and he used to take what was put in it.**

The traditional King James says, "the bag." The word *bag* in the original Greek literally is the word casket, and it means a "little box" that you put money in. The New King James calls it exactly what it was — a money box.

Now back to John 13:29:

For some thought, because Judas had the money box, that Jesus had said to him, "Buy those things we need for the feast," or that he should give something to the poor.

Now why would poor men think that a poor man like Jesus would be telling a poor man like Judas to give something to the poor? The apostles thought that Jesus said to go give something to the poor, because that was His modus operandi.

Judas had the money box. In our present day, a money box would be a treasury, and Judas would be the treasurer. The treasury is to hold what you have not spent. A treasury is for the purpose of holding surplus funds.

Jesus had a treasury, and a thief had stolen out of it for three and a half years. Not only was he stealing from the treasury, but he was stealing to the extent that none of the other eleven disciples knew that he was taking anything out of it. That tells us that there had to be an abundance in the treasury for no one to be aware that anything was missing. Jesus knew Judas was stealing by the Holy Spirit.

Another proof that Jesus was not poor was the fact that He called specifically twelve men into the ministry with Him. That means He was responsible for the maintenance of thirteen people, including Himself. He had to clothe them for three and a half years, because that was how long His earthly ministry lasted. He had to transport them, house them, feed them, pay their taxes, as well as provide for their families. That is, if they had any. Yet with all those expenses to be taken care of, there was still enough left over to give to the poor. If you can afford to take care of thirteen people and their families, you are in good shape.

I think we have blown a hole in the traditional concept of Jesus being materially poor. Jesus had plenty and so should you if you are serving God and living the Christian life.

We are trustees of the things of God. My question is, can you be trusted? Here is how you can find out if you can be or not. Ask yourself this question: What are you doing with what you already have? Do you save anything? Most people don't. They live up to everything they can get their hands on, but as soon as they get a raise, they go out and buy more things that devour that raise. I know this is so, because I have done it. But I am free now because I found out that the whole purpose of prosperity is for the proclamation of the gospel, but while the gospel is being preached, all my needs get taken care of just from the residual overflow.

You have to get to a point of godly satisfaction. When are you ever going to be satisfied? How big does your house have to be before you finally realize that your present house is more than adequate? We need to concentrate more on "seeking and saving that which was lost," as God wants us to do.

3

Obedience to God
Causes Us to Prosper

S ome people have found it hard to pull themselves away
from their money because they think it can do every
thing for them. The cemetery is full of people who would
have given every nickel they had if their money could have kept
them alive. For some people, including some Christians, their
money is everything, because they have been suckered in by
Satan to believing that there is nothing their money cannot do
for them. Money can do some things, but there are a lot of
things it cannot do. I want to cover a story in the Bible that
shows us what riches can and cannot do.

Mark 10:17-22:

> **17** **Now as He was going out on the road,
> one came running, knelt before Him
> and asked Him,** [Jesus never said a
> word to this man, nor did He search him
> out. The Bible says the man came
> running, not walking or jogging, but

41

running, and knelt before Him and asked Him this question:] **"Good Teacher, what shall I do that I may inherit eternal life?"** [This man was extremely perceptive. He didn't say, "Good teacher, how can I get eternal life?" He was wise enough to realize there was something he had to do to inherit eternal life.]

18 **So Jesus said to him, "Why do you call Me good? No one is good but One, that is, God."** [Jesus never asked him if he knew the commandments; He knew the man knew the commandments because he was a Jew, and all Jews knew them because they had to learn the Law of Moses at an early age.]

19 **"You know the commandments: *'Do not commit adultery,' 'Do not murder,' 'Do not steal,' 'Do not bear false witness,' 'Do not defraud,' 'Honor your father and your mother.'"***

20 **And he answered and said to Him, "Teacher, all these things I have kept from my youth."** [This man was something. He didn't say, "Well Lord, I followed a few of these things," or "I kept some of them." He said, *"All these I have kept from my youth."* Obviously, he was not still a youth because he said he had kept the commandments *from* his

42

youth, which would have meant about 12 or 13 years old.]

21   **Then Jesus, looking at him, loved him, and said to him, "One thing you lack: Go your way, sell whatever you have and give to the poor, and you will have treasure in heaven; and come, take up the cross, and follow Me."** [That the man only lacked one thing is pretty good. But notice what Jesus did not say, and many people miss this; He didn't say: "Go and sell everything you have and then give everything you get from what you sell to the poor." Probably the reason Jesus told the young man to sell *whatever* he had was because he could not drag those things around with him if he chose to follow Him. He would have had to turn them into liquid assets to travel easily with his wealth while on the road.]

22   **But he was sad at this word, and went away sorrowful, for he had great possessions.** [*For he had great possessions.* That is why he went away sorrowful. Because when Jesus told him to sell whatever he had, that meant those *great possessions* had to go, and he could not bring himself to do what Jesus said. I actually believe that this scripture is in-

correct; it should not read, *"for he had great **possessions."*** I believe it should read: "But he was sad at this word, and went away sorrowful, *for great possessions had him.*" And to illustrate that they had him, he could not give them up, not even for eternal life. I hear people all the time talking about having this or that habit that they cannot break. "I have this nicotine habit. I know, as a Christian, I should not be smoking these cigarettes, but I cannot seem to give them up." No, you don't have a cigarette habit; the cigarette habit has *you*. Some folk cannot stop smoking, even though it states on the pack of cigarettes that smoking can cause cancer. The only things you cannot turn loose are things that have you, such as drugs, alcohol, and sex. You do not have a sex problem; the sex has you. It has you jumping through hoops to the point where you cannot even think straight. It has you wrecking your life, and placing yourself in compromising situations where you could contract something that could kill you and destroy your family. You are out of control. That is where this man was. Great possessions had him, and Jesus perceived this about him by the Holy Spirit. That is why He told the man to sell all that he had.]

There may seem to be a contradiction between what I have been saying about prosperity and having material things. You may look at this passage and say, "See there. The Lord told that young man to get rid of his possessions." But there is really no contradiction. Jesus told the young man to sell what he had and give to the poor so he could locate himself. He did not do it so the man would *not* have possessions. We can figure this out from this statement: **"One thing you lack: Go your way, sell whatever you have and give to the poor."**

That verse shows us that God was not interested in the man getting rid of his possessions just for the sake of getting rid of them. If God wanted him to get rid of them, he would not have had to sell them. He could have simply given them away. Why have him take the time to sell things, trying to find a buyer and all of that, when he could have given them away?

The reason some Christians are not obedient to tithe is because they cannot conceive of giving God a portion of their hard-earned paycheck. They have forgotten — if they ever knew — that it is He who has given them the ability to get money in the first place. Just think of this: If Jesus suddenly appeared before you and said, "I need a thousand dollars right now," and you had a thousand dollars, would you give it to Him? Of course, in all probability your answer would be yes. But if you are not a tither, don't say you would because you wouldn't. If you won't give Him the 10 percent tithe, why would you give Him a thousand dollars?

Mark 10:23-26:

> **23   Then Jesus looked around and said**
> **to His disciples, "How hard it is for**

those who have riches to enter the kingdom of God!" [He did not say they could not enter. Jesus said simply noted that it was hard for them to enter in, just like that young man.]

24 And the disciples were astonished at His words. But Jesus answered again and said to them, "Children, how hard it is for those who trust in riches to enter the kingdom of God!

25 "It is easier for a camel to go through the eye of a needle than for a rich man to enter the kingdom of God." [Jesus never said the rich could not get into the Kingdom; He simply said it would be hard for them because they trust in their riches instead of trusting in God. It is not the riches that are at fault; it is trusting in them that cause the problem. Riches, money or wealth are neutral. It is what the person who has the wealth does with it that counts.]

26 And they were greatly astonished, saying among themselves, "Who then can be saved?"

The first time they were "astonished." Now, they are "greatly astonished." Why would they be astonished at the fact that rich people could not get into the Kingdom? They were probably thinking like most people think, that if the rich people cannot get in who is going to get in, because rich people can do anything they want? The apostles probably hunched one another and said, "Hey, Peter did you hear what Jesus said? He said it is easier for a camel to go through the eye of a needle than for the rich to get into the Kingdom. Man, Peter, if the rich cannot get in, how will the poor folk stand a chance?"

Mark 10:27-30:

27 **But Jesus looked at them and said, "With men it is impossible, but not with God; for with God all things are possible."** [Even getting a camel through the eye of a needle.]

28 **Then Peter began to say to Him, "See, we have left all and followed You."** [How could poor folk leave all? What *all* are poor folk going to leave? Unpaid bills? Foreclosure notices? Garnishments of their wages?]

29 **So Jesus answered and said, "Assuredly, I say to you, there is no one who has left house or brothers or sisters or father or mother or wife or children or lands, for My sake and the gospel's,**

30 **"who shall not receive a hundredfold now in this time — houses and brothers and sisters and mothers and children and lands, with persecutions — and in the age to come, eternal life.**

Peter was the one who said they (the apostles) had left all to follow Jesus, so I submit to you that they must have had some things to leave in order for Peter to say, *"we have left all."* The Bible does not tell us what the all was that they left, but obviously Jesus knew from when they first started traveling with Him. He knew what they left because He said, *"There is no one who has left house...."* Why would He say "left house" to someone who didn't have a house to leave? This statement had to be relevant to them. He said, *"house or brothers."* So, they must have had brothers and sisters, or a father and a mother or a wife and children and lands. Why would you say lands to someone who had no lands or property? How would it relate to them?

For My sake and the gospel's, who shall not receive a hundredfold....

I am probably going to get into a controversy here, but I do not think we yet know what *"for my sake and the gospel's"* means. The word *hundredfold* means one hundred times. In the past, I had used this scripture in reference to receiving a monetary gift and would often say to the giver: "I agree with you for the one hundredfold return." Well, now I believe this scripture cannot be used in that way, because that would mean that every time you give to someone who is either in ministry, or spreading the gospel, you should get back a hundred times more.

My wife and I, in the year 2000, gave $648 thousand into the Kingdom, and I figured it up. A hundred times that would be $64 million, eight hundred thousand! To this day, we have never received that much back.

I guarantee you that if it has ever happened to you, it only happened one time. No one I know of has ever given any money to the church and gotten back exactly one hundred times what they gave — at least, not on a regular basis. As I said, something might have happened miraculously at one time, but you don't get a hundred times back every time you give an offering in the church.

Here's the reason why: the hundredfold return has absolutely, positively nothing at all to do with money. I got this revelation in its final form while on my feet ministering on the subject of prosperity. Suddenly, it dawned on me — and I wanted to kick myself in the backside because I have read the scriptures dealing with this subject hundreds of times and never even saw it.

I even taught this series, *The Purpose of Prosperity*, where I talked about the hundredfold return, and I thought I had arrived at the point of great revelation on the subject. I even said to myself: *"Self, there is probably not too much more you can find out about this scripture on the hundredfold return."* That's why we can never afford to have the attitude that "I know that" or "I've heard that" when it comes to the Word of God. Just because you've read it or heard it before doesn't mean you know it.

Right in the scripture it tells you it is not about money, yet we've always thought that it was about money. I believe what I'm about to share with you will show you how to focus correctly on what the hundredfold is really about.

Let's look again at Mark 10:24-30:

24   And the disciples were astonished at His words. But Jesus answered again and said to them, "Children, how hard it is for those who trust in riches to enter the kingdom of God!

25   "It is easier for a camel to go through the eye of a needle than for a rich man to enter the kingdom of God."

26   And they were greatly astonished, saying among themselves, "Who then can be saved?"

27   But Jesus looked at them and said, "With men it is impossible, but not with God; for with God all things are possible."

28   Then Peter began to say to Him, "See, we have left all and followed You."

29   So Jesus answered and said, "Assuredly, I say to you, there is no one who has left house or brothers or sisters or father or mother or wife or children or lands, for My sake and the gospel's,

30   "who shall not receive a hundredfold now in this time — houses and brothers and sisters and mothers and children and lands, with persecutions — and in the age to come, eternal life."

Now where does it say anything about money in those verses? It seems to me that Jesus was very specific about what He referred to concerning the hundredfold. It doesn't say anything about money. Let's look at verses 28-29 again:

> **28 Then Peter began to say to Him, "See, we have left all and followed You."**
>
> **29 So Jesus answered and said, "Assuredly, I say to you, there is no one who has left...."**

Here is something the Lord showed me. Here is the key: It's in one little word.

Then Peter began to say to Him, "See, we have left..." Look at the word *left*. He didn't say we *gave* anything; he said we *left* something. **"... all and followed You."**

So Jesus answered and said, "Assuredly, I say to you, there is no one who has left...." He didn't say there was no one who has *given*; He said there was no one who has *left*.

Now here is the revelation: You don't leave money; you give money. He said **... there is no one who has left**, not *no one who has given*. You don't leave money; you give money. Even when you leave home, you take money with you. But you can't take the house with you. You have to leave that. You can't take your mama, necessarily, or your father or your brothers or your sisters, but you always take your money with you. He never said anything about giving. He said, "See, we have left." In fact, he said, "...we have left all." Then Jesus became very specific:

29   **So Jesus answered and said, "Assuredly, I say to you, there is no one who has left house or brothers or sisters or father or mother or wife or children or lands, for My sake and the gospel's,**

30   **"who shall not receive a hundredfold now in this time....**

So where does it say they "left money?" How do we have the right to put money in there, if Jesus didn't say it?

Let me take it a step further. If you look up the word *hundredfold* in *Strong's Exhaustive Concordance of the Bible*, one of the meanings is "one hundred times." But that is not how Jesus is using it. My God, who wants a hundred kids? You have trouble raising three. If I brought you 97 more kids on Monday, where would you put them? How would you feed them or clothe them or bed them down? Even if you had bunk beds you would have to have 50 of them. You don't have a house big enough for that.

None of us has ever received one hundred times the money we gave. Think about it and be honest. We've been giving for years and have never received a hundred times what we gave. If someone tells you that every time they gave a hundred dollars they got $10 thousand in return, they are lying through their teeth. They know it, and I know it.

In teaching on this hundredfold principle later at Crenshaw Christian Center, the church that I pastor, I asked whether there were any junior high, high school or college teachers in the audience. Several people responded. One woman, a high school teacher, raised her hand so I used her as my example.

Here's how the exchange went:

Me: "What do you teach?"

Teacher: "I teach high school."

Me: "How long have you been teaching high school?"

Teacher: "Twenty-eight years."

Me: "So that means you have had a lot of students come through your class. Have you ever given your students a test?"

Teacher: "Yes, many times."

Me: "Did the tests you gave over the 28 years have numerical value?"

Teacher: "Yes."

Me: "In all the tests that you have given, what is the highest numerical value that a student can usually make on a test?"

Teacher: "One hundred percent."

Me: "Can you other teachers agree with that?"

Other teachers: "Yes."

Me: "Well, I don't understand. Since one hundred is not as much as a thousand, why don't you give the students a thousand percent, or a million percent? They're a bigger percentage than a hundred. Why do you only give a hundred percent when you can give a million? Give the kid a thousand percent! Don't tell me that wouldn't encourage them and inspire them — *'Hey, I made a million on my test!'* That sounds better than a hundred. Where did you get the idea of a hundred?"

Now, I ask you the reader, where do you think this hundred came from?

53

Of course! It came from the Bible. It came from the hundredfold, and the hundredfold does not mean one hundred times.

Here is something else. The economy of the United States is not based on a thousand dollars or a million dollars? It is based on one dollar. There are one hundred cents in every dollar. One hundred cents! Our economy is based on one hundred cents — the stock market is based on it, and the other people in the world look at us and gauge us by those one hundred cents.

Some people think they want a hundred times everything, but they don't. Ask people who own a lot of property — it is a pain in the backside. You have to deal with tenants, trying to collect the rent, folk tearing up your property. Then when they don't pay the rent you have to get the sheriffs to evict them. It is more than a notion. You want a hundred? You can't handle what you've got.

And who in the world wants a hundred wives? Some men think they do. I know what some men think, *"What a way to die! If I've got to die — wow!"* But listen to what Solomon, the wisest man who ever lived, said. He had 700 wives and 300 concubines — one thousand women! Solomon came to the end and said, "Vanity of vanities. It's all vanity."

So my point is, it's not about money. It is an expression of a biblical principle. It's a figure of speech. All the hundredfold means is that you have reached the top of the scale. If I saw you in class and asked you, "What did you make on the test?" and you said, "One hundred percent," it tells me you got all the answers right. When Jesus used the term *hundredfold* He was simply saying that you made a hundred percent on the test. It does not mean a hundred times; it means you got one hundred percent right.

Now, this might sound like a contradiction, but I believe in the hundredfold return. I receive the hundredfold return all the time. But it is not a hundred times. It just means I made an "A" on the test. I made a hundred percent — that's all it means. Luke 6:38 validates that:

"Give, and it will be given to you: good measure, pressed down, shaken together, and running over...."

What more do you need? Why do you want to settle for a hundred?

And then if you bring all the tithes into the storehouse, God says He'll open the windows of heaven and pour you out a blessing. The last time He opened the windows of heaven and poured something out, it flooded the whole earth. Why are you going to settle for a lousy hundred percent when you can get the whole earth flooded with God's blessings? When God opens the windows of heaven, you will be inundated with blessings. The hundredfold is simply a value that means you can't leave anything for the Kingdom of God and His righteousness and come up shorthanded. That's all it is saying.

Let me show you a scripture — from the mouth of Jesus Himself — that puts the icing on the cake. You have to have somebody help you misunderstand this. Luke 18:28-30:

28   Then Peter said, "See, we have left all and followed You."

29   So He said to them, "Assuredly, I say to you, there is no one who has left house or parents or brothers or wife or children, for the sake of the kingdom of God,

30   "who shall not receive many times more in this present time, and in the age to come eternal life."

He doesn't use the word *hundredfold* here because what He means is *many times more*. What Jesus is saying to you is that you can't give up anything for the Kingdom of God that is going to make you come up short as a result. If you give up your house and you think you have given up something, God says you're going to get many times more in this present time. Not in heaven. Thank God for heaven, but we're not there yet. We're here.

Many times more — that's the idea. Jesus is simply saying to you that you can't beat God giving. It may sound trite, but it's a true statement. God won't allow you to beat Him at giving. He is not going to allow you to outdo Him. He is the Daddy, and He's going to let His kid outdo Him?

He said you would receive many times more, and sometimes that is what is necessary. People who are true missionaries leave mother, father, sister, brother, and some have left even the opportunity to marry to devote their lives to God. They left something. On the other hand, most people don't leave anything. God can hardly get them to go to church regularly, let alone leave their house for the sake of the gospel.

In fact, some have bought a bigger house. There is nothing wrong with that, but what I'm trying to say is that Peter and the other disciples did leave their homes. They were fishermen. They were businesspeople. They were not welfare recipients sitting by the welfare office with nothing to do when Jesus came along, saying, **"Follow Me, and I will make you fishers of men."** They were businesspeople with wealth and means.

They were the only people you could take out of the loop, as it were, and have them walking all over the countryside for three and a half years, leaving their wives and children at home while still being able to take care of them. It could only be someone who was independently wealthy whose family could live on the income and the interest from their businesses.

Jesus couldn't take poor folk and have them walking all over the countryside. How would their families eat? How would their children survive? He had to use people of means — businesspeople, fishermen, and tax collectors. In order to follow Jesus, they physically left their homes and their businesses. It said in Mark's Gospel that James and John left their father Zebedee in the boat and followed Jesus. They left something! Peter said we have left all to follow you. Jesus said they would receive many times more in this life.

But even if you leave a house, you are not going to get a hundred houses back. That's not what Jesus was saying. Remember what Peter said. Peter said, **"See, we have left all...."** In other words, they made a sacrifice. They left something to follow Jesus. What Jesus was saying is that there is no man who left anything that is going to lose out. But He didn't mean you were going to get a hundred houses.

I would suggest that you don't say what I said for years whenever I gave. That is, "I believe I receive the hundredfold return on my giving," because you are not going to get a hundred times the amount you gave. It's better to say, "I believe I receive the corresponding return." So whatever that is, I'm waiting to receive it. My hand is out. That way, you are in line with the Word of God.

The point is that the Lord doesn't really want us to give up anything. He needs a willing and obedient heart so He can give us the power to get wealth. If you are not willing, what is the point of giving you the power to get wealth to squander on your own desires or to keep in a bank account somewhere rather than making it available for the Kingdom to help establish God's covenant?

Like the young man we read about earlier, he had been obedient to follow the Law of Moses; that was how he got his *great possessions*. It would have been counter to the law, or the Word of God, for Jesus to tell the man to get rid of what he had received, because he had been obedient to God. I believe that if the young man had said, *"Okay, Lord, just give me a little time to go and sell what I have, then I will come and join You,"* that Jesus would have told him to keep his possessions.

What God needs from each of us is a willing heart. He does not need anything we have materially. We have nothing compared to what God has, because He owns the whole universe. Our little chump change doesn't mean anything to

Him, but He does need a willing and obedient heart to do His will in the earth realm. The young man wasn't willing. The Bible says he went away sorrowful because *great possessions had him.*

We are extensions of Jesus, because we are the body of Christ on earth. In other words, we are Jesus, for all practical intents and purposes. The world can only see Jesus as it sees Jesus in us. Since we are supposed to be hooked up to Him, we should be emulating Him. The Bible calls us *ambassadors* (2 Corinthians 5:20). It seems that most believers have forgotten that fact. Now, it is all about getting a new suit or a new dress or some new jewelry. We seem to have forgotten what the real issue of Christianity is about.

I pray that Christians will never be persecuted here in the United States. I pray that our government will not get overthrown so that we would have to go through what the people in Indonesia, Russia, China, or other countries have gone through. In America, we have it made in the shade. We are fat and increased with goods and think we have need of nothing. As the book of Revelation says, we do not realize that we are blind and naked (Revelation 3:17).

We have to get to a point of *godly satisfaction*, where we are freed up from financial bondage so we can be givers and channels through which Almighty God can bring the message of salvation to the world. That is why He has given the Church the power to get the wealth, not so we can stay in financial bondage and keep on paying 18 plus percent interest.

I am not trying to come down hard on the Church, but I want to stir the body of Christ into thinking about the wonderful privileges we have as Christians. We do not want anyone to mistreat us, yet we will mistreat God, our very best friend. Jesus is not going to the cross to die for anyone else. He has already saved everyone who is ever going to be saved. People have to come to know about the salvation Jesus has provided for them and be given the opportunity to accept and receive Him as their personal Savior and Lord.

We are the extension of Christ that must go into the world and tell people salvation is theirs for the receiving. We need both the *goers* and the *senders* to do this. We need a home base to launch the *goers*, and they should be completely unburdened of financial challenges. There is nothing intrinsically valuable about having to spend your life in some lowly place trying to win people to Christ while wondering if you are going to have something to eat each night. We, the Church, the body of Christ on the earth, need the wealth to get the gospel to the world. We are going to have to take God at His Word and get busy being *goers* and *senders,* establishing God's covenant and not following our own selfish goals and desires.

2 Corinthians 8:9:

For you know the grace of our Lord Jesus Christ, that though He was rich, yet for your sakes He became poor, that you through His poverty might become rich.

This *rich* versus *poor* is about tangible wealth, not spiritual wealth. If Jesus was rich spiritually and became poor spiritually, how could He save the human race? A spiritually poor man surely cannot help me, you, or anybody else for that matter, so

Jesus could not have been poor spiritually. This has to be talking about earthly wealth.

The words *poor* and *rich* are relative terms. A million dollars is a lot of money, but the newspapers today talk about a man who is worth 34 billion dollars. If you have only a million dollars, you are still poor in comparison to a man with 34 billion. When it says Jesus was rich but became poor, it is talking from the standpoint of heaven. The Bible says in heaven, the city is fifteen hundred miles square, and all the streets are made of gold. The city has twelve gates and all the gates are made out of a single pearl. So, when Jesus left heaven to come to earth, He became poor. Compared to heaven, all the wealth in this world would be like welfare.

How has Christ made us to prosper?

Galatians 3:13-14:

> 13 Christ has redeemed us from the curse of the law, having become a curse for us (for it is written, "Cursed is everyone who hangs on a tree"),

> 14 that the blessing of Abraham might come upon the Gentiles in [or through] Christ Jesus, that we might receive the promise of the Spirit through faith.

I would not debate it, but some people have interpreted that statement, *the promise of the Spirit,* to mean, "that we might receive the Holy Spirit, who had been promised to us." I think there is a deeper meaning to the statement. God gives revelation to mankind through the Holy Spirit, who is the only Person of the Godhead in the earth right now. As instructed by the Father, the Holy Spirit has brought to the earth realm the knowledge of God's plan and purpose for the ages. I believe the words *promise of the Spirit* are talking about what the Father said through the Spirit in reference to what belongs to us, the body of Christ, and what we ought to be doing with what belongs to us.

That the blessing of Abraham ....

This is an interesting statement. Who in the world is Abraham? And what has he got to do with anything? He did not go to the cross. He did not come down from heaven. He was not rich and became poor for us. What is this business about old Abe? Well, it turns out that Abraham is very important to the body of Christ because God wants us to understand the source for what we have or ought to have.

Let's explore the blessing of Abraham and what it has to do with the Christian.

Galatians 3:7:

Therefore know that only those who are of faith are sons of Abraham.

We know from the start that this has to be talking about something spiritual because Abraham is not our father. My mother was not married to Abraham. But God says that if I am of faith, I am a son of Abraham, so I need to know what that means.

62

Galatians 3:9:

So then those who are of faith are blessed with believing Abraham.

If I am blessed with believing Abraham, then Abraham must have been blessed in order for me to be blessed with him. The next question then would be, "If I am blessed with Abraham, how was Abraham blessed?" First, let's find out how Abraham was *not* blessed.

There is only one way anyone can come into a union with God, and that is through the Lord Jesus Christ. Jesus said in John 14:6, **"I am the way, the truth, and the life. No one comes to the Father except through Me."** Therefore, access to and contact with God has to be spiritual, through Jesus Christ.

Since this is true, Abraham could not have been spiritually united with God, since Jesus had not yet come to redeem mankind. From a technical/spiritual point of view, Abraham was not a Christian; therefore, God could not at that time be considered his spiritual Father.

Even though David followed God and wrote many of the psalms praising God, even though Solomon was a man called by God, and even though Daniel, Shadrach, Meshach and Abednego had an affiliation with God from the standpoint of believing that God was who He said He was, none of these men were Christians. In fact, from a spiritual point of view, they were all spiritually dead men, cut off from God.

That is why in the Old Testament there were so many supernatural physical manifestations of God's presence. That was the only way the Lord could relate to the people. He had to give them a pillar of cloud by day and a pillar of fire by night when he delivered the children of Israel from their Egyptian bondage, so they could see that God was with them. They could not sense His presence in their spirits because they were spiritually dead. We, as Christians, do not need physical manifestations of God's presence because He lives on the inside of us by His Spirit.

I believe that Abraham was not blessed spiritually in any way, form, or fashion, because he was a sinner, a servant of the Lord and not a child of God. There was only one way Abraham could relate to God, and that was materially and physically. When it says that we are *blessed with believing* or *faithful Abraham*, it means we are blessed *alongside* Abraham.

Now let's find out from the Bible how Abraham was blessed, so that there is no possibility of misunderstanding how we are supposed to be blessed, since we are to be blessed with him.

Genesis 12:1-3:

1   **Now the Lord had said to Abram: "Get out of your country, from your family and from your father's house, to a land that I will show you.** [God had not shown Abraham anything at that point. When God told him to leave, Abraham did not know where he was going. In essence, God told Abraham that He would show him where he was to go once he made the commitment to leave.]

2　**I will make you a great nation; I will bless you and make your name great; and you shall be a blessing.** [If God told Abraham, "I will make you a great nation," obviously Abraham could not have been a great nation when God first spoke to him, because God could not make him what he already was. Using that same rationale, apparently Abraham at that time was not a blessing to anyone.]

3　**I will bless those who bless you, and I will curse him who curses you; and in you all the families of the earth shall be blessed."** [This passage tells us that God is going to bless Abraham, but it does not specifically spell out whether or not the blessings will be spiritual or material. We still need to find out how Abraham was blessed so we will know how we are supposed to be blessed.]

Let's go to Genesis 13:1-2:

1　**Then Abram went up from Egypt, he and his wife and all that he had, and Lot** [Abraham's nephew] **with him, to the South.**

2　**Abram was very rich in livestock, in silver, and in gold.**

65

Thank God that the Holy Spirit put this statement in the Bible, so no unbelieving preacher, evangelist, or professor of theology could try to tell us that it is talking about spiritual blessings. It could not have been spiritual blessings, because Abraham was not even saved. The Bible says Abraham was very rich in livestock, silver and gold, but it still does not tell us that God gave him those riches. We assume that God did, but our assumption needs to be validated.

Abraham and Sarah had a son in their old age and the son was named Isaac. In those days it was the custom for parents to arrange marriages for their children when they came of marriageable age. In like manner, Abraham sent a trusted servant to a far country to his own relatives to pick a wife for Isaac. The servant took with him many treasures for the relatives. He then prayed that God would show him how to accomplish his master's bidding. Abraham evidently was a man over his house and taught his people, family and servants, the importance of prayer and trusting God.

The upshot was that the servant arrived at the place where Abraham's relatives lived. He stopped at a well where the young women were coming out to water the livestock. The servant prayed and asked the Lord to show him the right girl. In talking to one of the girls, the servant found out that she was a part of Abraham's family, and so she invited him to stay at their home. Let's continue on with the story where the servant arrived at the family home, beginning with Genesis 24:34-35:

34   So he said, "I am Abraham's servant.

35 **"The Lord has blessed my master greatly, and he has become great;** [Isn't that what God promised? And Abraham obviously told his servant about God's blessings. At first, Abraham's name was Abram, which means "father of the nation." God changed Abram's name to Abraham, which means "father of many nations," because He had told Abraham that He would make him the father of many nations.] **and He has given him flocks and herds, silver and gold, male and female servants, and camels and donkeys.**

So, if we are blessed with Abraham, then we ought to have silver and gold, and livestock too! The point is this: If we are of faith, we should have the same blessings Abraham had. What are our blessings for? They allow God to establish His covenant through us, to seek and save the lost.

If you do not think God knows what He is doing, if you do not think He has a purpose behind what He does, look at Ecclesiastes 10:19:

A feast is made for laughter, and wine makes merry; but money answers everything.

If you don't have any money, according to this scripture, none of your *everything* will be answered. So, God cannot be opposed to you having money. Let me show you how God blessed His servants who were obedient and faithful to follow

Him. If you can learn to trust God, then you can line up with His program and make yourself available to be a channel through which He can *seek and save that which was lost.*

As we cover the following scriptures, take notice that we are talking about people who were not saved, not even Spirit filled, nor did they speak with other tongues.

1 Chronicles 29:26-28:

> **26   Thus David the son of Jesse reigned over all Israel.**
>
> **27   And the period that he reigned over Israel was forty years; seven years he reigned in Hebron, and thirty-three *years* he reigned in Jerusalem.**
>
> **28   So he died in a good old age, full of days and riches and honor; and Solomon his son reigned in his place.**

Where do you think David got those riches? He got them from being a man after God's own heart.

2 Chronicles 1:7-12:

> **7   On that night God appeared to Solomon, and said to him. "Ask! What shall I give you?"**
>
> **8   And Solomon said to God, "You have shown great mercy to David my father, and have made me king in his place. [How did Solomon know how God had**

68

treated his father? Because David probably told him how God was with him when he killed the lion and the bear and the giant Goliath.]

9 **"Now, O Lord God, let Your promise to David my father be established, for You have made me king over a people like the dust of the earth in multitude.**

10 **"Now give me wisdom and knowledge, that I may go out and come in before this people; for who can judge this great people of Yours?"** [Notice, Solomon did not ask for success; he did not ask for riches, or the heads of his enemies; he asked for wisdom. Look at the magnanimous attitude of Almighty God, because of Solomon's heart to serve God by serving His people.]

11 **Then God said to Solomon: "Because this was in your heart, and you have not asked riches or wealth or honor or the life of your enemies, nor have you asked long life — but have asked wisdom and knowledge for yourself, that you may judge My people over whom I have made you king —**

12 **"wisdom and knowledge are granted to you; and I will give you riches and wealth and honor, such as none of the**

**kings have had who were before you,
nor shall any after you have the like."**

What is in your heart? Is seeking first the Kingdom in your heart? Is seeking to save the lost in your heart, or are you seeking houses, lands, vehicles, and clothes? What is in your heart?

4

How God's Wealth
Is Transferred to Us

God placed wealth in the earth realm. The diamonds and the rubies and all that we call precious metals were created by God. The question is: "How do we, the Church, get the wealth into our hands so that we can establish God's covenant on the earth?" You cannot get it by working a 9-to-5 job. Yes, you ought to work to meet your needs, but just working will not get you ahead of the game. There are just a handful of folk that make it by working, and usually they are the ones with specialized talents or abilities. The system is not designed for the average person to get ahead to where he or she is freed up to be a financial channel through which God can work to bring forth His covenant.

There is no shortage of wealth in the world system, but Satan is not going to give up readily any wealth to those who are seeking to save the lost. He does not want the lost sought, and he certainly does not want them to come into the knowledge of God's Word. He has to figure out ways to keep the wealth from getting to us, and he has developed a clever system for doing just that. He keeps raising the prices on everything, so people are barely able to make it. That is why Jesus tells us in Matthew 6:19-21:

> **19** "**Do not lay up for yourselves treasures on earth, where moth and rust destroy and where thieves break in and steal;**
>
> **20** "**but lay up for yourselves treasures in heaven, where neither moth nor rust destroys and where thieves do not break in and steal.**
>
> **21** "**For where your treasure is, there your heart will be also.**"

Whenever we hear the word *treasures*, we immediately think of gold, silver, diamonds, rubies, and sapphires — the things we believe make up wealth. But how can we lay up gold and silver in heaven? How are we supposed to get precious gems into the heavenly bank? These verses are not telling us not to have an earthly bank account or not to put money away. They are talking about where your heart and your treasure are. In the book of Ephesians, it says we are blessed in the heavenly places.

Ephesians 1:3:

Blessed be the God and Father of our Lord Jesus Christ, who has blessed us with every spiritual blessing in the heavenly *places* in Christ.

The word *us* in this scripture is referring to those of us in Christ — Christians. In Matthew, we are told to lay up for ourselves treasures in heaven, because where our treasure is, there our heart will be. Geographically speaking, heaven is in the spirit world. God has blessed us with every spiritual blessing. We have to understand that everything that is material was first of all spiritual before God called it into physical existence. Gold, silver, rubies, diamonds, and emeralds had to be in the mind of God before He physically created them. These things were first in heavenly places because they were first in God. Then when God said, *"Let there be,"* God spoke these things into what we know as a three-dimensional physical world. But everything in the physical world was first in the spirit world, because God, who is a Spirit, created the physical world.

The Bible tells us, **In the beginning God created the heavens and the earth** (Genesis 1:1). Therefore, the Creator had to exist before the creation could come into existence. Since God is a Spirit, and He created the three-dimensional physical world, then the three-dimensional world had to already be in God before He spoke it into existence. So when He spoke He knew that what He spoke was what He had on the inside of Him.

For example, before our church sanctuary, the FaithDome, was built, the architects first had to do the plans of what we wanted. They developed plans of the structure, as well as computer-generated drawings as to what the building was going to look like when it was finished. But the building first had to be in the mind of the architect before the plans and drawings were done. These dome builders construct domes all over the world, basically for storage purposes, but we had them design our dome to be a church. Once the structure was built, we had to compare the building plans and the computer-generated drawings with the structure itself to be sure we had in physical existence what was in the plans.

Well, just as the architects had to have the FaithDome in their minds before it was built, God had the world in Him before it was created. He spoke out what was in His mind and it came into physical existence. So, when God says, **…who has blessed us with every spiritual blessing…**, the Holy Spirit through the Apostle Paul is letting us know that everything we will ever need in the physical world is already in existence in the spirit world and on deposit for us in the heavenly bank.

Now by faith, we extract from the heavenly bank and bring those things that we need or desire into the three-dimensional physical world so that we can utilize them for the fulfilling of God's covenant to seek and to save the lost.

Making Deposits Into the Heavenly Account

There are two primary ways of making deposits into the heavenly account. The first way is by tithing, and the second way is by investing in the gospel. I want to deal with tithing first because it is the primary channel by which God is able to bring wealth to us. There is a law that God placed in the universe from the very beginning. It is called the *law of sowing and reaping.* It is impossible to reap if you have never sown. You cannot receive any dividends if you have never made any investments.

The biggest tax write-off the average person usually has is the purchase of a home. Most home purchases are on a 30-year mortgage. In a few rare cases, it may be less. Because most of what you pay on the house note goes toward interest the first few years, the interest amount can be deducted from your income tax.

Can you imagine how many people have died and gone to hell in 30 years? Homeowners get to write off the interest, and usually, that is the biggest single write-off or exemption they will have. But you can get the same benefit by giving to God as you can by writing off interest on a mortgage. In fact, you get a double blessing. When you pay mortgage interest and write it off, all you get is an exemption. If you tithe, you get the same exemption. In other words, you don't have to pay taxes on your tithe, just as you do not have to pay taxes on the interest you pay on your house. But when you tithe you have sown seed into the Kingdom, and that causes the windows of heaven blessings to come back to you.

Back in 1977, I bought a house. I wanted to be free to be a giver. I wanted to give into the Kingdom, but I was tied up with bills like everyone else. But Betty and I got our bills under control and bought this house. I determined that this was going to be the last house I was ever going to buy. But everything was based on where I was at that time in my life and what I knew. I had no idea back in 1973 that the ministry of Crenshaw Christian Center would grow to be as large as it is, or that we would be on television.

My wife and I wanted to be free to give into the Kingdom, so we believed God and by using our faith — the same principles of faith that I have been teaching people for over 30 years — we paid off a 30-year mortgage in three and a half years. We then were financially free to give as much as we could, beyond our regular expenses, into the Kingdom.

As I said, the ministry grew far beyond anything we ever imagined. And then God told me to go on television. All of a sudden I became recognizable just about everywhere I went. We would have people come and literally camp out in front of our house, taking pictures and waiting for us to come out. We would watch the people going by looking at where we lived. I had special shades installed where we could see out but no one could see in. We could hardly come out of the house without finding somebody waiting to take a picture of someone in my family or me. It was crazy. My children became especially concerned and said, "Daddy, you have to move someplace more private." It sort of became harassment, and we just got tired of it. So we decided to buy another house. We needed a place that would give us a little seclusion, and yet not be too far away from the church. The upshot of the thing was that the Lord gave us a beautiful home, very protected, in a secluded area, but it cost 21 times more than what the other house cost.

Here we were back into making house payments again. I had been believing and confessing that one day someone would give me $1 million. I confessed that for over thirteen years, and one day it happened. It paid off our mortgage, so that we were once more free of house payments. By believing God and using our faith, we paid off that house 20 years ahead of time. We no longer have to make interest payments or house notes, and that money now can go toward seeking and saving the lost.

God knows our hearts, so you might wonder, *"Well, I'm tithing, and I'm giving and I'm making all the right confessions, but it doesn't happen for me like it happens for Pastor Price. He keeps giving these testimonies about how people just give him money all the time. I go to the same church, study the same Bible. I believe the Word. I confess the scriptures, but it doesn't happen for me like that."*

It could be that God cannot afford to let it happen to you because He knows all you are going to do is go down to the new car dealership and buy an expensive car, or a van, or something else you really don't need. You are not going to give it towards the gospel or for seeking the lost. The Bible says it is God who gives us power to get wealth. So, since God is the One who gives the power to get wealth, He has a right to give it to whomever He wills. I am not saying this is the reason it is not happening for you, but it is a sobering thought. Perhaps, you need to check your heart out.

Have you ever wondered why Jesus said to lay up for yourselves treasures in heaven and not here on earth? After all, He knows very well that we cannot send dollars to heaven. I believe Jesus told us to do this because if your heart is where your treasure is, and if your treasure is where your heart is, and your heart and your treasure are in God, your treasures are not subject to earthly conditions. Everything in this earth realm is subject to earthly changes.

A few years ago, banks were paying 13, 14 percent interest. When you got your bank statement, you would see you had made a bundle that month. The banks do not pay that kind of interest any more because the situations in the financial community and banking systems have changed. The financial institutions may be paying 14 percent one year and go down to 5 percent the next year. On earth, the value of money fluctuates. People need much more money now to do the same things they did 10 years ago. But if your treasure is in God and your heart is in God, it doesn't matter whether the interest rates go up or down. You know that your treasure is secure because God has an economy that never changes.

Tithes and Offerings — How God Pipes Wealth to Us

It is amazing to me how much misunderstanding there is about tithing. Some people can understand and interpret the most intricate details of daily living, but when it comes to giving to the Lord, they get all confused. Paying tithes to God is giving Him 10 percent of your financial income, whatever that income is or wherever that income comes from.

Before God created the universe, He already had to be God and was always in existence. The Bible says that **in the beginning God created the heavens and the earth** (Genesis 1:1). Therefore, the heavens and the earth are the result of God's creative act. My point in saying this is to emphasize the fact that God does not need the universe to be God. He did not need the heavens and the earth to come into existence to be God. And He does not need us, the human race, to be God. He would still be just as great and awesome as He has always been and always will be.

Tithing is not for God's benefit; it is for our benefit — the Church. Many people feel as if tithing is unfair, saying, "I don't understand why God wants my money. Tithing does not seem right to me and I don't see why I need to give God 10 percent." You don't have to; God will not make you tithe. That is another important thing to understand. God will not make you give or do anything. He is not asking us to give so that He can have; He is asking us to give so that we can have.

In order to participate in tithing, you have to know that it is God's will, and it is God's methodology for us in these times. I say this because some people believe that tithing was under the Law, and that as Christians under the New Testament it is not necessary for us to tithe. That is not true, biblically speaking. Tithing was actually instituted before the Law was given, and we see this in Genesis 14:1-20:

> 1   And it came to pass in the days of Amraphel king of Shinar, Arioch king of Ellasar, Chedorlaomer king of Elam, and Tidal king of nations,
>
> 2   that they made war with Bera king of Sodom, Birsha king of Gomorrah, Shinab king of Admah, Shemeber king of Zeboiim, and the king of Bela (that is, Zoar).
>
> 3   All these joined together in the Valley of Siddim (that is, the Salt Sea).
>
> 4   Twelve years they served Chedorlaomer, and in the thirteenth year they rebelled.

5   In the fourteenth year Chedorlaomer and the kings that were with him came and attacked the Rephaim in Ashteroth Karnaim, the Zuzim in Ham, the Emim in Shaveh Kiriathaim,

6   and the Horites in their mountain of Seir, as far as El Paran, which is by the wilderness.

7   Then they turned back and came to En Mishpat (that is, Kadesh), and attacked all the country of the Amalekites, and also the Amorites who dwelt in Hazezon Tamar.

8   And the king of Sodom, the king of Gomorrah, the king of Admah, the king of Zeboiim, and the king of Bela (that is, Zoar) went out and joined together in battle in the Valley of Siddim

9   against Chedorlaomer king of Elam, Tidal king of nations, Amraphel king of Shinar, and Arioch king of Ellasar — four kings against five.

10   Now the Valley of Siddim was full of asphalt pits; and the kings of Sodom and Gomorrah fled; some fell there, and the remainder fled to the mountains.

11   Then they took all the goods of
      Sodom and Gomorrah, and all their
      provisions, and went their way.

12   They also took Lot, Abram's brother's
      son, who dwelt in Sodom, and his
      goods, and departed.

13   Then one who had escaped came and
      told Abram the Hebrew, for he dwelt
      by the terebinth trees of Mamre the
      Amorite, brother of Eshcol and
      brother of Aner; and they were allies
      with Abram.

14   Now when Abram heard that his
      brother was taken captive, he armed
      his three hundred and eighteen
      trained servants who were born in his
      own house, and went in pursuit as far
      as Dan.

15   He divided his forces against them
      by night, and he and his servants
      attacked them and pursued them as
      far as Hobah, which is north of
      Damascus.

16   So he brought back all the goods, and
      also brought back his brother Lot
      and his goods, as well as the women
      and the people.

17   And the king of Sodom went out to
       meet him at the Valley of Shaveh (that
       is, the King's Valley), after his return
       from the defeat of Chedorlaomer and
       the kings who were with him.

18   Then Melchizedek king of Salem
       brought out bread and wine; he was
       the priest of God Most High.

19   And he blessed him and said:
       "Blessed be Abram of God Most
       High, Possessor of heaven and earth;

20   and blessed be God Most High, Who
       has delivered your enemies into your
       hand." And he [Abram] gave him
       [Melchizedek] a tithe of all.

I covered all of that to get to the word *tithe*. Technically the *tithe* means "one-tenth," or as we would say "10 percent." Abraham lived 430 years before the Law was given to Moses by God on Mount Sinai. Yet, Abraham gave Melchizedek a tenth, or 10 percent. Why didn't he give him 15 percent or 12 percent? Where do you think Abraham got the idea of a tenth?

Genesis 28:10-22:

10   Now Jacob went out from Beersheba
       and went toward Haran.

11   So he came to a certain place and
       stayed there all night, because the

sun had set. And he took one of the stones of that place and put it at his head, and he lay down in that place to sleep.

12 Then he dreamed, and behold, a ladder was set up on the earth, and its top reached to heaven; and there the angels of God were ascending and descending on it.

13 And behold, the Lord stood above it and said: "I am the Lord God of Abraham your father and the God of Isaac; the land on which you lie I will give to you and your descendants.

14 "Also your descendants shall be as the dust of the earth; you shall spread abroad to the west and to the east, to the north and the south; and in you and in your seed all of the families of the earth shall be blessed. [This is a continuous prophecy God originally gave to Abraham, that carried over to Isaac and then to Jacob].

15 "Behold, I am with you and will keep you wherever you go, and will bring you back to this land; for I will not leave you until I have done what I have spoken to you."

16   Then Jacob awoke from his sleep and said, "Surely the Lord is in this place, and I did not know it."

17   And he was afraid and said, "How awesome is this place! This is none other than the house of God, and this is the gate of heaven!"

18   Then Jacob rose early in the morning, and took the stone that he had put at his head, set it up as a pillar, and poured oil on top of it.

19   And he called the name of that place Bethel; but the name of that city had been Luz previously.

20   Then Jacob made a vow, saying, "If God will be with me, and keep me in this way that I am going, and give me bread to eat and clothing to put on,

21   "so that I come back to my father's house in peace, then the Lord shall be my God.

22   "And this stone which I have set as a pillar shall be God's house, and of all that You give me, I will surely give a tenth to You."

Where do you suppose Jacob got his idea of a tenth? I tend to think that he picked it up from his father Isaac. Isaac probably tithed also, although the Bible does not record that he did. But we know his father Abraham tithed. Since the Law was not in force and would not be for 430 years, where do you think Abraham got the idea of giving a tenth?

I believe tithing has always been God's *modus operandi*, and it probably started in the garden of Eden. I cannot prove this, but God is consistent, and Abraham had to get the knowledge of tithing from somewhere. Since God doesn't copy man, then God could not have gotten the idea about tithing from man; it would have to be the reverse. God is the same, yesterday, today and forever (Hebrews 13:8). If He were ever for the 10 percent, or tithe, He will always have to be until He has finished His work of redemption.

Malachi 3:8:

"Will a man rob God? Yet you have robbed Me! But you say, 'In what way have we robbed You?' [God speaks and says:] **In tithes and offerings."**

God is speaking to Israel at this time from a dispensational point of view, but how could God be fair and accuse people of robbing Him if they did not know what to do to keep from robbing Him? So, if He said to the Israelites: "You have robbed Me in tithes and offerings," they had to already know about tithes and offerings.

I submit to you that tithing did not originate with the Law, but God incorporated it into the Law in order that those under the Law could be blessed by it. So Christians cannot use the excuse that tithing is not for the Christian today because it was a part of the Law. Tithing originated before the Law, became a part of the Law, and is still in effect today.

As a Christian if you are not tithing, the Bible says that you are a God-robber, because the tithe belongs to the Lord. In other words, a robber is a thief. One who is a thief takes something that does not belong to him or her. When God says that we have robbed Him in tithes and offerings, it means that before we robbed Him the tithes and offerings belonged to Him. The only way we can be guilty of robbing God is by taking something that belongs to Him. What we have to understand is that everything in the world belongs to God, because He created everything. When you create something, whatever you create is yours. The wealth of the world belongs to God by right of creation, and when we don't give the Lord His share of what He financially provides for us, we are robbing Him. According to the Bible, we are God-robbers.

Many Christians do not understand this fact. Some even think that when they give their tithes and offerings to a church, they are giving their money to the preacher or the local church, instead of realizing they are giving to God what belongs to Him. This is why some Christians expect the church to bale them out of their situations when they get into a financial bind. They say, *"Well, I pay tithes here and I feel the church should give me my money back or loan me the money I need."* They do not realize that the tithe is the Lord's and when they paid their tithes and offerings they were giving the Lord only what was due Him. The church receives the tithes and offerings on behalf of the Lord for the work of the ministry, but the tithe belongs to Him. Now a church may decide to help someone out, but it is not because of the tithe, but rather because of the heart of the church.

A tither pays the tithe 12 months of every year, 52 weeks of every year and 24 hours a day. In other words, a tither tithes all the time. If you don't tithe all the time, then you are not a tither. You are just someone who now and then gives 10 percent. You cannot be a tither for six weeks and not be a tither the seventh and eighth weeks. To make it as plain as I can: if you are not consistently or regularly giving God your tithes and offerings, you are not a tither and you are robbing God and incurring the curse.

I wish the Internal Revenue Service would follow God's example and only tax me 10 percent. God has never raised the ante on tithing. It has always been 10 percent, and it is still 10 percent today. If you are not giving 10 percent, you are not tithing. Tithing is not an offering; it is an obligation that is used for our benefit, because God has everything He needs. He doesn't need our money.

Tithing is the first method by which God gets the wealth to us. We cannot use the world system as a guide in reference to the things of God because the world system is dominated by Satan. And he is doing everything he can to keep wealth out of the hands of the children of God. I went to Malachi to show that the Jews knew about tithing and that it did not originate with the Law. Now let's go back to Malachi and cover the scriptures that have to do with the principles of giving tithes and offerings.

Malachi 3:8-10:

    8   **"Will a man rob God? Yet you have robbed Me! But you say, 'In what way**

have we robbed You?' In tithes and offerings.

9   [God tells them:] **You are cursed with a curse, for you have robbed Me,** *even* **this whole nation.**

10   **Bring all the tithes into the storehouse, that there may be food in My house, and try Me now in this," says the Lord of hosts, "If I will not open for you the windows of heaven and pour out for you** *such* **blessing that** *there will* **not** *be room* **enough** *to receive it."*

This is one of the few times in the Bible where Almighty God comes down on man's level when He tells us to "try" Him, or as the traditional King James says, "prove" Him. You want to find out if there is a God? "Prove" Him by tithing and see if He will not pour out for you such blessing that you will not have room enough to receive it all.

I can tell you from experience that tithing works. I have been tithing for more than 30 years, and I have never missed one single time in tithing since I started. I am not bragging about this, because this is what I am supposed to do, and as a Christian, you are too. I tithe because I want to be obedient to my heavenly Father, and I decided more than 30 years ago to "try" Him. I have found out that what He said about the windows of heaven blessing is absolutely, positively true!

I want to point something out about Malachi 3:10:

"...and try Me now in this," says the Lord of hosts, "if I will not open for you the windows of heaven and pour out for you *such* blessing that *there will* not *be room* enough *to receive it*."

Notice that the word *there* is an italicized word, which means that the word was not in the original manuscript. Also note that the words *will, be, room, to, receive, it* — all are italicized, meaning that they were added by the translators.

The original text would read this way: "pour out for you such blessing that not enough." What is not enough? The blessing is not enough. I don't know what the translators' thinking was, but according to that scripture the blessing the Lord will pour out if we are obedient to tithe will not be enough, so that He will just have to keep on pouring out more and more and more until it is enough. That is great news in and of itself, but look at Verse 11:

"And I will rebuke the devourer for your sakes, so that he will not destroy the fruit of your ground, nor shall the vine fail to bear fruit for you in the field," says the Lord of hosts.

We need to translate this verse into our present day and time to get a full understanding of what it is saying to us today. We are not an agrarian or farming society. Most of us do not farm or till the ground as the children of Israel did. We work at various jobs — many of them highly technical — that pay us money for the services we provide.

We know from other scriptures that the devourer is Satan. He's the one who some people do not believe exists, but just because they don't believe he exists does not take him out of existence. It just means that they are being scripturally stupid. Jesus believes the devil exists, or else why would He say in John 10:10: **"The thief** [and a thief is definitely a devourer] **does not come except to steal, and to kill, and to destroy."**

Notice Malachi 3:11 again: **"And I will rebuke the devourer for your sakes...."** This is the only place in the Bible where God says that He will do something about the thief. Everywhere else when it talks about the devil, we are commanded to do something about him.

Don't think the devourer will come dressed in a red suit, holding a pitchfork in his hand, with a long pointed tail and horns. No, he comes in through unpaid bills, sickness that robs you of your health, marital problems that rob you of your peace of mind, and other challenges of daily living — all designed to devour you and your well being.

That is what the devourer will do, and some believers are losing the battle because they have been consistently robbing God. It is not that God is punishing them. He doesn't have to because there is a curse involved for those who are not tithing. It is bad enough to be cursed, but the curse is compounded, because Verse 9 says: **"You are cursed with a curse."**

Adam let the curse into the earth realm in the garden of Eden, and it has been on the earth since that time. If you walk in line with God's Word, then you are protected from the curse and its ability to impact your life. The moment you rob God or get out of line with the Word, you get over into where the curse is, and it can come upon you and wipe you out.

There is an insurance company called Travelers Insurance whose trademark is a red umbrella with rain falling on the umbrella. Under the umbrella, of course, there is no rain. The company's motto implies that if you stay under their umbrella of coverage, you are protected from the rains of adversity. The rains of adversity are falling all the time; insurance doesn't stop the rain from falling, but it stops it from falling on you and wiping you out.

The curse of adversity is falling all the time like the rain, but if you stay under the protection of God's Word, it doesn't stop the rain from falling, but it does stop the rains of adversity from falling on you. When you rob God by not tithing, you are not under the protective umbrella of God's Word. You're on Satan's turf, and he will blow you away. And the thing that is so tragic about it is that once you get out from under the umbrella God cannot protect you because you are out of His safety zone. It is extremely easy to stay in God's safety zone — just obey the Word.

If you are openly living in sin, your faith cannot work; your confessions are empty, useless and pointless. And even if you are tithing and giving for the support of the Kingdom, the enemy has a right to eat up your seed because you are not living in line with the principles of the Word. You cannot be in the will of God with tithing and out of the will of God with your life or in His will with your life and out of His will in tithing. You have to have it all together if you want the blessings of God on your life.

For example, you may or may not know this, but the body of Christ is not under the Ten Commandments, because we are not under the Law. We are under grace. But some of the Ten Commandments say thou shalt not kill, thou shalt not steal, thou shalt not bear false witness, thou shalt not make any graven images of anything or the likeness of anything in heaven above or in the earth beneath. Now even if you keep all nine commandments and end up stealing, you have broken the Law — not the law of stealing. You have broken the whole Law because there is only one Law that has 10 divisions to it.

By the same token, you cannot live any way you want, then pay your tithes, and think it is okay with God. If you are living in open rebellion against the Word, you can give a million dollars a week and it will not mean a thing. Following the Word is a total life, and you cannot pick and choose the parts you want to obey. Your life is extremely important because your life is supposed to mirror what you are on the inside. Whatever is in your heart will be seen through your life.

The Book of Revelation refers to books being opened. Those are record books. There are actually records being kept on everyone of us, and the reason those records are being kept is so that when we stand in judgment, the way we have lived will be there for us to see. We won't be able to say, "I didn't do this, that or the other." The records will bear out how we have lived our lives, and God's computers never go down.

Let's look at Malachi 3:10 again, I want to point out another important point on tithing.

Bring all the tithes into the storehouse...

One of our ministry employees came up with the suggestion of having the tithes deducted from employees' paychecks, just as credit union, car note, and other deductions are done. I am absolutely against this because God says in Verse 10 to **"bring all the tithes into the storehouse."** He did not say, *"Let someone take the tithe from you."* We have to understand that it is not just about the money. It is about being disciplined and obedient to what God has instructed us to do. If you are not disciplined in paying your tithes yourself, you are probably not disciplined in anything else. It takes discipline to succeed in life. It takes discipline to walk by faith and not by sight, and how can you learn discipline if someone takes your tithes and sends them in for you?

To me it is the greatest blessing to be able to pull out my checkbook and write a check for the amount of my tithes, fill out the offering envelope, and get it ready to put into the offering container when it is passed to me. I relish this process because I am saying when I do this: *"Father, I honor You; I worship You with this act of faith. I am separating me from that which I earned through the labor, the sweat, as it were, of my brow. I am giving this to You Father; I'm paying my debt to You gladly, happily. Thank You for blessing me so much that I can do it."*

Notice that God says the people were robbing Him of tithes and offerings. We do not owe the offering. It is something that is given voluntarily. A tithe is what is owed. The curse comes from not tithing, and not from holding back an offering. But we should give offerings. (I will cover offerings in more detail later, but I wanted to make this point about the offering not being owed.)

Tithing Is the First Way God Blesses Us

Over the years that I have been a pastor, I have shared a lot of personal things with my congregation because this is the way the Lord has led me to teach. Basically, I am a very private person. I wouldn't even tell my name unless I was forced to do it. When I am teaching, I am very animated and talkative. Ordinarily, I don't do that much talking. But the Lord dealt with me about sharing some personal matters in my life, because people need to know that He works the same today as He did many years ago. It is wonderful to read about people who lived 2,000 years ago being tremendously blessed by God, but we need to see people today in our time who have been just as blessed so that we can be inspired and encouraged to trust God as those who lived so long ago.

I remember when I first found out about divine healing many years ago. Before that time, the churches I belonged to did not teach anything about divine healing. In fact, they said healing went out when the last apostle died. But I found out that God is still in the healing business, and that He still wants to heal us and make us well. So I took every opportunity to stand against anything that would come against my physical body. Then one day I heard a man say that he had not been sick in 37 years — had not even had a headache in 37 years. When I heard that, something went off on the inside of me, and I realized that divine healing is great, but divine health is best! So, I began to use my faith for divine health. Some people may have thought the man was bragging, but I knew he was giving a testimony of God's faithfulness and what has been provided

94

for us through Jesus Christ. That testimony inspired me to use my faith for divine health.

So, I began to share some things about our personal life, particularly about our finances, to encourage and inspire others. When my wife and I attained certain goals, I would let the congregation know, "We're tithing 15 percent now." Then we went to 20, and then to 25 percent, and now 31 percent of our total income goes into the spreading of the gospel. A tithe is only a tenth. But using the percentage principle as a guideline we say we tithe 31 percent. We still give offerings over and above the 31 percent! I am not telling you this to brag, but to encourage you to be obedient to the Word. God will not fail you; you can trust Him. Giving 31 percent leaves 69 percent for us to live on, but because of God's faithfulness; we live better on the 69 percent than we could if we kept the 100 percent while robbing God. It was while we were tithing 25 percent that the $1 million came to pay off our house.

In some Christian families, the wife is working and the husband is working two jobs, and they still do not have enough money coming in to live on and to tithe. I know because I did that when I was robbing God in years gone by. I could not get a handle on anything. I don't care how much money I made, it seemed never to be enough. It got so bad for me that I had to declare bankruptcy.

I could not pay the bills. They even repossessed the television, the car, and called back all the credit cards. Me — a minister of the gospel — bankrupt! I loved God with all my heart, but I was operating in that curse and did not even know it. I thought I could not get ahead because I am black. That was an easy way out. It had nothing to do with color; it had to do with obeying God. When you obey God, you get into the stream where the blessings flow. I have been tithing now for more than 30 years, and I can tell you it is worth it to be obedient to God's Word. You can trust God with that 10 percent. In fact, you are doing yourself a disservice if you don't.

It is not right to not pay your debts in order to tithe. When you do that your witness is not good. If you signed a contract and told the people you were going to pay X-number of dollars every month, you have to stand behind your word. If you renege on your bills, you can never witness about Jesus to those to whom you owe money.

The first thing you need to do to get out of debt is to stop charging. Stop buying, and put every effort and every penny into getting to a point where you can get out of debt. That is what I had to do. We had so many bills it was ridiculous. I was out of control. I was like a junkie; I had three monkeys on my back and each monkey had two little monkeys on his back. If you have to declare bankruptcy, you are in bad shape. I found out that it does not pay to walk in the curse, so I made every effort to get out of it, and I have never been back, and I never will go back.

I have had some people, who attend my church, come to me and say, *"Pastor, I used to tithe, but then I got in over my head financially and stopped tithing. Now I need to get back to tithing, but I'm still having financial problems."* This is where we see through a glass darkly; this is where we know only in part. The Bible does not give a clear-cut answer to such situations. Let me share with you what Betty and I did, and what I think people might do to get into a position to tithe if they have never tithed before, or return to tithing if they have stopped.

There are two basic scenarios concerning tithing versus paying bills. The first scenario is a person like I was who did not know what tithing was about when he first came to the Lord. I had heard the word *tithe*, but the context in which I heard it involved a pastor coming up with a gimmick to get people to give their money. He would preach on tithing in such a way that it would put the people on a guilt trip, or either it would scare them so much that they expected God to drop a bomb on them any minute. There was never an explanation given about the purpose or benefits of tithing.

In many instances, when Christians find out about tithing, they have already fouled up their finances. They already owe their souls to the company store, and are having difficulty meeting all their financial obligations. These are people who need to get themselves out from under their debt before beginning to tithe. That was how it was for my wife and me years ago. We could not afford to tithe and pay all of our bills. We could not save any money, because I wasn't making enough. In addition, I was out of control when it came to spending. I had gotten my family in so much debt that when we found out about tithing, there was nothing we could do about it. However, I really wanted to tithe because I wanted to please my heavenly Father.

What I decided to do was to let Uncle Sam save my money for me. I went to the payroll department where I worked and changed the status of my dependents for income tax purposes. I claimed no dependents for one year. At the end of the year, I claimed all of my dependents and my other deductions. I got some money back in one lump sum as an income tax refund. Instead of splurging with the refund, I paid off a bill that was commensurate with what my tithe would be, based upon my income at that time. I traded that bill for the tithing process. I started tithing from then on, and I have never stopped since.

Let's look at the scenario concerning a person who was a tither but stopped because of financial problems. This person knows about tithing and the purpose and benefits of tithing, but for some reason allows himself to become financially extended beyond what he is able to pay. I believe such a person needs to tithe first before paying the bills. Here is why: He was already tithing before he got so financially strapped that he could no longer pay both their financial obligations and the tithe.

He needs to tithe because those obligations that caused him to dip into God's money makes him a thief, spiritually speaking. He is robbing God, and may be robbing the businesses he owes, as well. There is no doubt he is in a bad situation. But it is better to be in debt to the people he owes than to rob God. All he will get from owing bills are penalties and late notices, but if he robs God, he is going to be cursed with a curse!

I am not telling you to cheat people and not pay your bills; you have to pay your obligations. As a Christian, you are expected to be a person of integrity and honor your commitments. You may do some damage to your credit rating, but if you have already been tithing, then paying your tithe is your first obligation. You may need to contact your creditors and explain that you intend to pay them; it just may take longer than you (or they) expected.

We are under the honor system. God is trusting us with His money. Why would you want to steal God's money, knowing He is the One who saved you and filled you with His Holy Spirit? He is the One who heals you when you get sick, and provides for you when things go bad.

There is no reason for people to steal from the tithe. I know some people might say, *"Yeah, but suppose an emergency comes up? Two tires blow out at the same time. I have to get to work. Or Hurricane Floyd came through and blows off the top of the house. We have to have a roof over our heads."* Yes, that is true, but the tithe money doesn't belong to you. And even if you take the money to make needed repairs, you are still a thief. If you did not have the money, you could not use it, could you?

What you have to do in order not to rob God is to change your way of thinking about money. That is what I had to do to keep from taking God's money. Now, I don't care if the car blows up; I don't care if the roof comes off the house, and the walls fall down. That is no excuse to take the Lord's money. How can you be blessed and get your house fixed with stolen goods? If you robbed a bank to put a new roof on your house, do you think God would bless you? He could not because the money is stolen. It is the same thing when you take the tithe from the Lord.

You hear people say diets don't work. That is a lie. Any diet will work, but the key to achieving results from a diet and keeping the weight off is to change your attitude about eating. Do you think the devil came into your bedroom in the middle of the night while you were sleeping and put 15 pounds on you? No, of course not. Generally speaking, people do not gain weight in the process of not eating. It is the easiest thing in the world to lose weight – stop eating to excess! The weight will come off, but in order to keep it off, you have to change your attitude about food.

The point I am trying to get across is that you have to change your attitude about what belongs to God: 10 percent belongs to God and 90 percent belongs to you. You have to think in terms of 90 percent. So when you sign a contract to pay installments of any kind, you cannot obligate yourself past 90 percent because that is all that you have to work with. Again, 10 percent belongs to God, 90 percent belongs to you, and that makes 100 percent.

If you have trouble with paying your tithe, what you might do is to open a separate bank account. That way you can keep your money separate from the Lord's, and whenever it is time to pay your tithes, the money is there. I know this is more burdensome, but it is one way of making sure you don't steal the tithe. You do not need to be out of control. You are a child of God. You have the Holy Spirit (or you should have), so you ought to be in control.

Proverbs 3:9-10:

> **9   Honor the Lord with your posses-
> sions, and with the firstfruits of all your
> increase;**

100

10 **so your barns will be filled with plenty, and your vats will overflow with new wine.**

The **firstfruits of all of your increase** is talking about the tithe. In other words, the tithe comes off first – off the top! You don't tithe from what is left over. You live on what is left over. If you do not see it that way, you are not seeing it properly, because there will never be enough left over. The devil, through the circumstances and through the system, will see that there is not enough. He will try to do his best to make sure that there is nothing left so that there is nothing with which to seek those who are lost. If your barns are filled with plenty, then you will have plenty to sow into seeking and saving that which is lost.

One of the things the Lord said to the children of Israel was that if they would be willing and obedient, they would eat the good of the land (Isaiah 1:19). A lot of people are willing, but they are not obedient. Being obedient includes tithing, as well as living right, and through your obedience to tithe, you put yourself in a position for God to pipe His blessings to you.

You may be wondering why you have had it so hard financially and why you have not been able to make it as you should. Well ask yourself this question: *If you were God, would you trust you?* Knowing you like you know you, if you were God, would you put a lot of confidence in you? God is about winning the lost. He wants you to be blessed, but His first priority is seeking to save that which was lost. That is His purpose for our prosperity.

5

Our Partnership With God

The way we actively partnership with God in seeking the lost is through bringing in the tithes and offerings. It all starts with a willing heart and a desire to be obedient to the One who has given so much for us.

Deuteronomy 26:1-2:

> **1**   **"And it shall be, when you come into the land** [the Promise Land] **which the Lord your God is giving you as an inheritance, and you possess it and dwell in it,**

> **2**   **"that you shall take some of the first of all the produce of the ground, which you shall bring from your land that the Lord your God is giving you, and put it in a basket and go to the place where the Lord your God chooses to make His name abide."**

In this Old Testament scripture, God is speaking to the children of Israel, as they were on their way to the Promised

Land. I want to zero in on the first verse because we want to look at its counterpart in the New Testament.

Colossians 1:13:

He has delivered us from the power [domin-
ion] **of darkness and conveyed us into the kingdom of the Son of His love.**

The Kingdom that we are in is comparable to the land that the children of Israel had been promised. They had been in severe physical bondage and suffered many things for many years, but were now liberated from their physical chains. Christians, as children of God, have been delivered from spiritual bondage and the power of darkness and conveyed into the Kingdom of God. We did not have to cross the Jordan River or fight the giants in the land to get our freedom, but we have a land that belongs to us — and all because of Jesus Christ, our Savior and Lord.

Deuteronomy 26:2-3:

2 **"that you shall take some of the first
of all the produce of the ground, which
you shall bring from your land that
the Lord your God is giving you, and
put it in a basket and go to the place
where the Lord your God chooses to
make His name abide.**

3 **"And you shall go to the one who is
priest in those days, and say to him,
'I declare today to the Lord your God**

> **that I have come to the country
> which the Lord swore to our fathers
> to give us.' "**

The basket, or collection container, of the local church is the place where the Lord has made His name abide. Let's look at the New Testament counterpart Hebrews 3:1:

> **Therefore, holy brethren, partakers of the
> heavenly calling, consider the Apostle and
> High Priest of our confession** [profession],
> **Christ Jesus.**

The Old Testament people had a high priest, and they brought their offerings in a basket and presented them to the high priest, or to the priest of those days, in the place where God chose to place His name. We have a High Priest, the Lord Jesus Christ, who abides in the holy sanctuary of heaven. When we take our tithes and offerings to the local church and place them in the offering baskets or containers, we are actually "bringing" them to the Lord Jesus so that He can set them before the heavenly Father on our behalf.

Hebrews 6:17-20:

> **17   Thus God, determining to show more
> abundantly to the heirs of promise the
> immutability   of   His   counsel,
> confirmed it by an oath,**

> **18   that by two immutable things, in
> which it is impossible for God to lie,
> we might have strong consolation,**

who have fled for refuge to lay hold
of the hope set before *us*.

19   This *hope* we have as an anchor of
the soul, both sure and steadfast, and
which enters the Presence *behind* the
veil,

20   where the forerunner has entered for
us, *even* Jesus, having become High
Priest forever according to the order
of Melchizedek. [Isn't that interesting
that Melchizedek was the one that the
patriarch Abraham gave a tithe to 430
years before the Law?]

Let's see something else about Jesus receiving our tithes
and offerings and presenting them to God on our behalf. By the
way, for the benefit of those who think that tithing is not mentioned in the New Testament, the scripture we are about to
read mentions tithing eight times!

Hebrews 7:1-9:

1   For this Melchizedek, king of Salem,
priest of the Most High God, who met
Abraham returning from the slaugh-
ter of the kings and blessed him,

2   to whom also Abraham gave a
tenth [1] part of all, first being translated "king of righteousness," and
then also king of Salem, meaning
"king of peace,"

3   **without father, without mother, without genealogy, having neither beginning of days nor end of life, but made like the Son of God, remains a priest continually.**

4   **Now consider how great this man was, to whom even the patriarch Abraham gave a tenth [2] of the spoils.**

5   **And indeed those who are of the sons of Levi, who receive the priesthood, have a commandment to receive tithes [3] from the people according to the law, that is, from their brethren, though they have come from the loins of Abraham;**

6   **but he whose genealogy is not derived from them received tithes [4] from Abraham and blessed him who had the promises.**

7   **Now beyond all contradiction the lesser is blessed by the better.**

8   **Here mortal men receive tithes [5], but there He** *receives them* ["them" refers to tithes, 6]**, of whom it is witnessed that He lives.** [The writer is talking about Jesus in this verse. In other words, Jesus is in heaven at the right hand

of the Father. When we bring our tithes
to mortal men (the local church pastors
or ministers), Jesus receives those tithes
and presents them to the Father on our
behalf.]

9   **Even Levi, who receives tithes** [7],
     paid tithes [8] **through Abraham...**

Let's go back to Deuteronomy 26. It contains something that is very important with regard to making a confession when presenting the tithe.

Deuteronomy 26:3-11:

3   **"And you shall go to the one who is**
     priest in those days, and say to him,
     'I declare today to the Lord your God
     that I have come to the country which
     the Lord swore to our fathers to give
     us.' [Under the New Testament, we
     Christians should go before the Father
     and declare that we are in the land that
     God gave us through our Lord Jesus
     Christ. That is what the above scripture
     indicates we can say when we bring in
     the tithes. In other words, we should not
     just bring the tithe, but we should make a
     confession that we have been delivered
     from the power of darkness and are in
     the Kingdom of God when we present
     our tithes to the Lord.]

4   **"Then the priest shall take the basket out of your hand and set it down before the altar of the Lord your God.** [This lets us know that there should be some time spent in presenting our tithes and offerings. In Malachi it says to "bring" all the tithes into the storehouse — not send them in. One of my parishioners said to me, "Pastor, I work on Sundays, so can I send my tithes in?" And so I answered and said, "You mean to tell me you cannot ever come to church? You work seven days a week, twenty-four hours a day? You don't have to bring your tithes to a Sunday morning service. That is the ideal time, but you ought to find some time to bring in your tithes. We have several midweek Bible studies and services. If you positively have no other way of doing it, you can bring your tithes to the church office any time it is open and say, **"I'm bringing my tithe and I'm declaring that I am in the land which the Lord God has given to me. Here is my tithe, take it and put it in the basket and present it to my Lord to be set before my God."**]

We have many people who watch our television program, *Ever Increasing Faith,* and who actually consider our program to be their church. They have not found a church in their area where they can learn the Word, so they send their tithe to us. In this situation, because they do not live close to the church, they have to send in their tithe. However, I always encourage these people to try to find a church near them where they can fellowship with the saints, as well as "bring" in their tithes.]

5   **"And you shall answer and say before the Lord your God: 'My father was a Syrian, about to perish, and he went down to Egypt and dwelt there, few in number; and there he became a nation, great, mighty, and populous.**

6   **'But the Egyptians mistreated us, afflicted us, and laid hard bondage on us.**

7   **'Then we cried out to the Lord God of our fathers, and the Lord heard our voice and looked on our affliction and our labor and our oppression.**

8   **'So the Lord brought us out of Egypt with a mighty hand and with an outstretched arm, with great terror and with signs and wonders.**

9   **'He has brought us to this place and has given us this land, "a land flowing with milk and honey";**

10   **'and now, behold, I have brought the firstfruits of the land which you, O**

Lord, have given me.' Then you shall set it before the Lord your God, and worship before the Lord your God.

11   **"So you shall rejoice in every good thing which the Lord your God has given to you and your house, you and the Levite and the stranger who is among you."** [This confession pointed backward to the children of Israel's bondage while they were in Egypt and to their deliverance, and then to where they were when they were making their confession, free and unchained from their past. They were reminding themselves of where they had been and where they were now. When people do that, they have a better appreciation of where they are now.]

At Crenshaw Christian Center, we do a similar acknowledgment of our deliverance when we present our tithes and offerings to the Lord based on the scriptures in Deuteronomy 26. While holding up our tithes, as if placing them in the hands of Jesus, we make this profession of our faith:

Heavenly Father, we profess this day to You, that we have come into the inheritance, which You swore to give us. We are in the land, which You have provided for us in Jesus Christ, the Kingdom of Almighty God. We were sinners serving Satan; he was our god. But we called upon the name of Jesus, and You heard our cry, and delivered us

110

from the power of darkness and translated us into the Kingdom of Your dear Son.

Jesus, as our Lord and High Priest, we bring the firstfruits of our income to You, that You may worship the Lord our God with them. Father, we rejoice in all the good which You have given to us and to our households. We have heard Your voice and have done according to all that You have commanded us.

Now Father, as You look down from Your holy habitation from heaven, to bless us as You said in Your Word, we believe that we now receive those blessings according to Your Word. This is our confession of faith, in Jesus' name. Amen.

We do not make this confession just to fill up the time of the service. We are following the commandment of the Lord. We have tailored the confession for the New Covenant dispensation. We don't just stuff money into an envelope; we bring the tithes and offerings with respect and love to God. We bring them in with joy and in remembrance that what we used to be, we are not anymore. We have been redeemed from the curse of the law; we are the head and not the tail; we are above and not beneath, and we are blessed coming in and we are blessed going out. This is how we, as children of the Kingdom, should bring our tithes and offerings.

Faith and Tithing

To understand the importance of exercising faith when we tithe, let's look once more at Malachi 3:10:

"Bring all the tithes into the storehouse, that there may be food in My house, and try Me now in this," says the Lord of hosts, "if I will not open for you the windows of heaven and pour out for you such blessing that there will not be room enough to receive it."

Under the New Covenant, the word *food* is talking about spiritual food. When Satan came to tempt Jesus in the desert, telling Him to turn stones into bread, Jesus replied, **"It is written, 'Man shall not live by bread alone, but by every word that proceeds from the mouth of God' "** (Matthew 4:4).

The Bible is God's mouthpiece in the earth realm, and it should be taught in every church that names the name of Jesus. If all you get from going to church on Sunday is a sweet pill of emotion and you are not learning how to walk in the power of the Word of God, then you are being robbed of the food that you need to develop your spirit man.

God says, "try Me in this." What is very important to understand when you try God is that you are going to have to use your faith to receive the blessing God wants to pour out on you, or else the thief (Satan) will steal it before it gets to you. As long as you are a Christian, you will never get away from having to walk by faith. It is not a matter of bringing in the tithe only. You have to do something else to get the benefit of your obedience.

Not only do you have to come with the confession of your mouth, but you also have to take a stand daily and say, *"I believe I receive my return on my tithe (or offering) and devil you cannot touch my return. I bind your power in the name of Jesus; I stand on the Word of God and I believe I receive my return."* Then the windows of heaven blessing will get to you.

God said He was going to do two things: (1) open the windows of heaven and (2) pour out for you a blessing. But you have to do the receiving part and you have to do it by faith. You may say, *"Well, I have been tithing and it has not gotten me anything."* If you know you are living right, it could be you are not using your faith. It may be you are just doing it as a legal spiritual obligation, but you are not really exercising faith to receive the return. If there is no faith exercised, the devil will steal the benefits of your tithing from you. We have to bring in the tithe and then claim the return; that is the way God has designed the system to work.

You may hear different preachers saying different things. As it says in 1 Corinthians 13:12: **"For now we see in a mirror, dimly…."** We do not see things from a spiritual perspective perfectly, because we are not perfect. We only know in part, but thank God for the part we do know. Don't get hung up and strung out on the fact that different ministers say different things. Let me explain this further:

Some ministers will say, *"You pay your tithe at all cost. You pay your tithe even if you don't pay your bills."* We really can't find anything in the Bible that says yea or nay on that premise. Let me give you my view. Then you see what makes sense to you.

I have had people at my church who say to me, *"I used to tithe, but then I got in over my head financially, so I stopped tithing; now I need to get back to tithing."* But they are still financially strapped and they really do not have enough money to pay all their obligations, plus tithe. Still, they feel they should tithe. What I believe they should do is to work to get rid of those bills, at least one bill and replace that bill with tithing — if the dollar amounts are equal. Then from that point on they should continue to tithe and not make any more bills beyond what they are able to handle and still tithe.

What Is the Purpose of the Storehouse?

Under the Old Testament economy, there was no such thing as a church as it is known today. However, there was a temple, which belonged to all the people. In the course of their lifetime, all the Jews were admonished to make a pilgrimage to the temple at some point. Inside the temple, shut up behind the Holy of Holies was the Shekinah Glory, the very presence of Almighty God. The Holy of Holies was behind the great veil. Once a year, the high priest would enter the Holy of Holies.

In the temple, there was a place called the treasury, or the storehouse. Under the Old Covenant, those who followed God were called servants of Jehovah. (These people could not be born again, because Christ had not died yet to provide redemption, which is why they were called servants of God rather than sons of God.)

God had the temple erected to represent His presence among the people. They could see the temple and they could see the high priest arrayed in his special garments to serve in the temple. God had to do this visibly because He was dealing with spiritually dead people who were cut off from Him because of the sin of Adam and Eve in the Garden of Eden.

The priests who took care of the temple did not work the land as the people did. The priests primarily took care of the temple and ministered to the Lord on behalf of the people. In order that the priests' physical needs would be taken care of, as well as the needs of the temple and its surrounding grounds, God had the people bring their tithes to the treasury, or storehouse.

As we have mentioned, the Israelites were an agrarian society primarily. They worked the land, and everything they had came from their labor of the soil or animal husbandry. They would bring corn, grain, pressed olive oil, milk, hides and fat from the animals, and the animals themselves to the storehouse for the care of the priests and the temple. In addition, the high priest would disseminate to the strangers, widows, and orphans who could not fend for themselves food and other items from the storehouse as the people needed.

What Is the Purpose of the Church?

Under the New Covenant, God does not deal with us on a three-dimensional level. He deals with us in the Holy of Holies on the inside of us — our spirits. Because of what Jesus did on the cross — reconciling God to man and man to God — there is no longer a veil covering the Holy of Holies or a human high priest who, as under the Old Covenant, was the only person who had the right to enter the Holy of Holies and talk to God.

When Jesus was on the cross, and in His last hour of life, the Bible says Jesus cried out with a loud voice saying, "Father, into Your hands I commit My spirit" (Luke 23:46). Then He bowed His head, and gave up His spirit. As His life was ebbing from Him, the veil in the temple was rent, or torn in half from top to bottom, indicating that the veil blocking the way to the Holy of Holies was taken away. The people no longer needed an earthly priest to get to Almighty God. Now, we can go directly into the throne room of God by virtue of what Christ did at Calvary (Hebrews 4:16).

A church building is not a temple. It is simply a place where the temples come together to fellowship around the Word of God and with one another, and to bring in the tithes and offerings. God lives on the inside of us; He doesn't live in a church building. Do you think that when a church service is over and the people go home, that God sits there in a chair and waits until the next time His children come together? No, He goes out when we go out of the building, and He comes in when we come in.

Because there are so many people in the world today as compared with the number at that point in Israel, and there are more Christians than there ever were Israelites, God has to have a channel by which He can funnel the wealth that He gives us the power to get. Ministry now is spiritual; it is not physical. It is not wrong if the local congregation agrees to feed poor folk who do not have anything to eat. It is not wrong if the congregation agrees to clothe people who do not have clothes to wear. But that is not the purpose of the church. It is good to feed the poor and to clothe the naked, and these things could be a bait to draw some people in so that they can be ministered to. That is what we do at Crenshaw Christian Center through our Community Outreach Program, but that is still not the primary purpose of the church. The Church that Jesus set up was not to be a welfare agency. It was to be a channel through which He could pipe the wealth so that the lost could be sought and brought into the knowledge of Him.

What Is the Purpose of the Tithe Today?

God tells us to tithe because that is how He provides the financing to seek and save that which is lost. We have local congregations so that everyone can go to a church somewhere. There is no building on earth big enough for all of the Christians to get into, so we have places where local people can gather and we call them churches. But in fact, there really is only one Church.

Tithing is a spiritual transaction, even though the tithe that we bring in is a physical thing that comes out of our income, which is usually obtained from labor. Instead of bringing in cows, sheep, chickens, eggs, corn, wheat and such as a tithe, we give our increase in dollar amounts. Through those dollars, we are able to disseminate spiritual information through different Christian channels so that the lost can find out about the gospel and get saved.

We do not have storehouses, per se, as under the Old Covenant, though we could say that the local church is the storehouse as compared to the temple under the Old Covenant.

The word *storehouse* implies a place where something is stored for future use. In other words, a storehouse is designed to hold something that cannot be consumed right now, so it has to be stored for use at another time or at a later date. The local church is where God meets with His people through the ministry gifts that He set in the Church (Ephesians 4:11). God views the local congregations as sheepfolds. And so He places over these sheepfolds, shepherds. The New Testament word *pastor* literally means shepherd.

The shepherd is responsible for ensuring that the sheep and lambs are cared for. Since this is a spiritual transaction, the sheep and the lambs are fed a steady diet of "spiritual food," which is the Word of God. Spiritual food (the Word) is stored in the storehouse in the care of the shepherd to be issued (taught) to the sheep and lambs for spiritual development and growth. The Word of God is the only food that the recreated spirit man requires. The traditional King James says "meat in my house." You should be able to go to any local church and find food, or meat. If there is no spiritual food for you to eat, then you have no right putting God's money (the tithe) into that storehouse. Now if you do not think it is important to God where you put the tithe, let me show you a passage of scripture that will knock your uppers out of their place.

There are many Christians who still think that the tithe belongs to them, so they take the tithe and break it up and send a little here and a little there, and a little everywhere. They send some of the tithe to *Ever Increasing Faith*, some to the Christian Broadcasting Network, and some to the Trinity Broadcasting Network. In other words, they divide the tithe. That is wrong. You can only have one storehouse or, rather, you should only have one. You cannot serve two masters; you cannot take care of two or more storehouses. You should only take care of

118

one. You should find that place that is a storehouse for you, where you can receive the Word of God to feed your spirit man. That is where your tithe should go. Now if you want to take from the 90 percent that belongs to you, then you can send a little bit here, a little bit there, and a little bit everywhere. That is your money, and you can do anything you want with it. But you have to make a value judgment about where to put God's money. Remember, the tithe is not *your* money. It belongs to God, and you are only a trustee of it. Let me prove this to you in the Bible.

Deuteronomy 26:13-14:

13   **"then you shall say before the Lord your God: 'I have removed the holy tithe from my house, and also have given them to the Levite, the stranger, the fatherless, and the widow, according to all Your commandments which You have commanded me; I have not transgressed Your commandments, nor have I forgotten them.** [In other words, they were doing what God commanded them to do under the Old Covenant.]

14   **'I have not eaten any of it when in mourning, nor have I removed any of it for an unclean use, nor given any of it for the dead. I have obeyed the voice of the Lord my God, and have**

done according to all that You have commanded me.' "

Now let me show you Verse 14 in the Amplified Bible.

I have not eaten of the tithe in my mourning [meaning you moaning, "Woe is me, I can't pay my bills; I have too many bills so I am going to use the tithe money."] **[making the tithe unclean], nor have I handled any of it when I was unclean, or given any of it to the dead; I have hearkened to the voice of the Lord my God, and have done according to all that You have commanded me.**

If you go to a church where they do not teach you how to walk by faith and not by sight, that is a dead church. If you go to a church, and they do not teach you about divine healing, that is a dead church. If you go to a church and they do not teach you about being filled with the Holy Spirit and speaking with other tongues, that is a dead church. If you go to a church and they do not tell you about prosperity and that God wants you to be blessed going out and blessed coming in, that is a dead church. If you cannot go to your local church and get healed, that is a dead church.

And if you take God's tithe and put it in a church that is not teaching and preaching the full-counsel of God according to the Word of God, you are giving it for the dead. You had better be careful what ministries you give to — even your own 90 percent. If the church is dead, it ought to be buried, and we need to have a funeral for it.

Where Should You Pay Your Tithes?

You need to find out if the local church you attend is teaching the Word of God, and if there is life there. If all you are getting is some traditional doctrine about what men have to say, you are not going to be able to grow in the things of God. If you are not being taught in church what the Bible says, then you are not being fed but you are being starved spiritually because you are not receiving any spiritual nutrition.

You should be able to go to church and learn how to live a victorious Christian life, and not just get a good feeling on a Sunday morning, or at a special musical program. If all you are getting is a good feeling and nothing to carry you through from Monday through Saturday, that is a dead church, and you should not be putting God's tithe there.

Twenty Percent Penalty for Stealing the Tithe

If you had been tithing and for some reason (usually because of a financial bind) you stopped tithing, then when you start tithing again, there is a penalty that has to be paid for the time you did not tithe.

Leviticus 27:30-31:

> 30 " 'And all the tithe of the land,
> whether of the seed of the land *or* of
> the fruit of the tree, is the Lord's. It
> is holy to the Lord.

31 **'If a man wants at all to redeem any**
of his tithes, he shall add one-fifth [20
percent] **to it.' "**

This is called the penalty clause. When you pay back the
money you stole from God, you are supposed to pay 20 percent interest. The purpose is to, hopefully, discourage you from
stealing God's money. Not only do you become a God-robber
again, but once more, you are operating under the curse. The
moment you miss tithing, you are back in the curse. What people
have to get into their heads, is that the tithe is God's money,
and He is serious about His money. The way you stay away
from the negative effects of the curse is to operate in the principles contained in the Word of God. When you are diligent to
do that, even though the curse is falling around you, it cannot
touch you.

Things You Cannot Use the Tithe For

You cannot buy Christian materials with the tithe and call
that tithing. *"Well, I'm buying Christian tapes, Pastor. In
fact, I'm buying your tapes."* You are still a thief. You cannot
buy Christian books, or even a Bible, with God's money and
call that tithing.

Tithing From the Net or the Gross

In Old Testament days, the people did not have what
we call net and gross. Basically, they always tithed from their
gross, because they did not have any tax as we do today. They
had to pay taxes, but not as we do. In today's economy, the

average working person is under the net and gross system. The gross means the total amount of money you make. The net is the amount you have left over after deductions are taken from your paycheck. Let me use myself as an example.

Ministers of the gospel are considered self-employed. I have to pay my own income taxes. The church pays me a salary, but it does not take out any payroll deductions for me. So my net is my gross. If I get $1,000 a week, I take 31 percent of that right off the top as my tithe, pay my taxes and any other voluntary deductions I choose to make.

If the company you work for takes out payroll deductions, such as federal and state taxes and Social Security benefits, and such, you have no control over those deductions. They are, in fact, mandatory deductions, and you do not even see that money because it goes immediately to the agencies making the deductions. You do not tithe from the total amount of your check; you tithe from what you receive after those mandatory deductions are taken out. For example, say you make $1,000 a week and the company takes out $250 as deductions, leaving you with $750 as your net income. You would tithe from the $750.

Once I was out of work and had to get unemployment insurance benefits. When I received my checks from the State Unemployment Office, I would tithe from those checks, because I now had control over them. For people like myself, who are considered self-employed, and you have to pay your own taxes, you tithe from the gross, because your net is your gross. It is the same if you are receiving Social Security benefits. You tithe from the total amount you receive, because now it is your money, and you have control over it.

Let's look at another scenario. Let's say you work on a job that has a credit union, and you decide to buy a car through that credit union. You have to pay tithes on the amount deducted for the credit union, because that is not a mandatory deduction, but one you elected to have taken out yourself. If you decided to buy a car outside of your credit union, you would pay tithes because it is just another bill that you incurred on your own. It is the same way with the credit union car.

Having a Heart to Tithe

Sometimes there are situations where one spouse wants to tithe, and the other spouse is not in agreement. While teaching this series, I received the following letter, which illustrates such a situation:

Dear Dr. Price:

I am married with three small children. I'm saved and filled with the Holy Spirit. My husband is not. Since you began the current series, "The Purpose of Prosperity," I have purposed in my heart to tithe and have been regularly tithing on my income only each month. Due to the fact that my husband and I were not good stewards of our income before I began coming to CCC, we have poor credit and late paying history. My question is now that I know the purpose of my income and in light of the problems my husband and I must financially overcome, what am I to do? My husband's solution is for me to stop tithing and use that money to help us pay off our debt. I know he has a valid point, but my solution would be to sell our '98 car and get a much older smaller car for half the payments, cut out buying lunch at work and anything else we can cut out so that I can continue to tithe, and we can get back on track with our finances.

I truly take the Word seriously and I have been blessed above and beyond since beginning to tithe. At the same time, I have read in the Bible where it says that the husband is the head of the wife and I must respect him. I'm concerned that if I stop tithing, I will be going back on my promise to God and will be cursed with a curse. It is my goal to be obedient to God and His Word and to respect my husband that I may be an example, which God may use to lead him to God.

I am sure there are many Christians who find themselves in similar situations. Because this dear lady obviously has a heart for God and wants to do right in paying her tithes, I believe God will honor her desire to tithe. The Bible does say that the wife is to be in submission to her husband (Ephesians 5:22), so she is doing right by submitting to him, and God will honor her for showing him respect. But they, as a family, should make every effort to pay off their debt. In the meantime she could tithe from the allowance she gets from the family income, if there is such an allowance. This way her Christian witness will not be compromised with her husband or the people they owe.

She should be also in diligent prayer for her husband to get saved and to have the wisdom to understand the importance of tithing and being in God's perfect will.

Giving Offerings — Investing in the Gospel

Tithing is the primary way we partner with God in financing the Kingdom; the giving of offerings, or investing in the gospel, is the second way. In other words, tithing and investing in the gospel, which would be classified under general offerings, are the methods through which God will pipe the wealth to us to seek and to save that which was lost.

Tithes are not offerings, and offerings are not tithes. You pay a tithe, but you give an offering. You give God 10 percent and you get to keep the 90 percent, from which you make offerings.

In talking about the offering, I want to re-read Mark 10:29-30:

> **29 So Jesus answered and said, "Assuredly, I say to you, there is no one who has left house or brothers or sisters or father or mother or wife or children or lands, for My sake and the gospel's,**

> **30 "who shall not receive a hundredfold now in this time — houses and brothers and sisters and mothers and children and lands, with persecutions — and in the age to come, eternal life."**

126

I dealt with this in some degree before when I talked about the hundredfold return. Now I want to talk about the second method by which God gets the wealth to us. Don't ever think you are going to lose by giving to God or giving for Jesus' sake and the gospel. You will always get back more than you gave — that is, if you give with a willing heart. If you give to God grudgingly, you will not get anything back because you will not be giving in faith. You will be giving out of a sense of obligation, and that does not please God. God wants to partnership with you so that He can bless you, and not just get your money. If only we could grasp that fact, how much further along the body of Christ would be. In the following scripture, you can plainly see it is God's desire to bless us, but we have to do something first.

Luke 6:38:

"Give, and it will be given to you: good measure, pressed down, shaken together, and running over will be put into your bosom. For with the same measure that you use, it will be measured back to you." [The flip side would be *don't give, and it will not be given to you.* It is very simple. You do not have to be a rocket scientist to understand this principle.]

I found that in order to receive big, I have to give big. That is why I give big. If you don't like what you have been receiving, just check up on what you have been giving, because what you give controls what you receive in the Kingdom of God. That is the way it works. Money is not going to drop into your hands out of the sky. It will come through the hands of men.

My wife and I are constantly giving. When we hear about a genuine need, we just get our checkbook out and write a check to help a brother or a sister out. We have a lot of seed going into the ground all the time. I keep on sowing and keep on reaping; keep on giving and keep on receiving — that is how it works.

The Great Commission

Jesus tells us in Mark 16:15: **"Go into all the world and preach the gospel to every creature."** There are multitudes of people around the world who have not yet heard the gospel. Some people act like the body of Christ is only for us in America. We are supposed to sit around church, get fat on the Word, enjoy the choir and praise the Lord. No, the local church is supposed to be a staging area. The local church is supposed to be where the resources and funds, through the tithes and offerings, should come in so we can pool those resources to send the *goers* out to seek and to save that which was lost.

We need to be able to send those who are willing to go first class! Here is why: We are not just wanting to see men saved, but see them saved and brought up to a level that God would have them walk in. We want to send out *goers* in such a way that they make a double impact — not just in proclaiming the gospel but also representing what they preach.

If God calls you to go, He will give you the grace to go. Don't ever worry about the Lord sending you somewhere you do not have a desire to go. God is never going to make anyone go where he or she does not want to be. There are enough challenges with the person who wants to go. He does not want to have to fight with someone who does not want to go. All God needs is a willing heart, that says: *"Lord, here am I; send me in whatever way You want to send me. If it is for me to be a goer, I'm willing to do that. If you need a man (or woman), I'm Your man (or woman). I know that if You have called me, You will give me the grace to do it. You will give me the ability to do what You have called me to do, and You will give me the anointing to be able to do whatever needs to be done."*

Look at how important the *goers* are to the proclamation of the gospel, but *senders* are just as important, because the *goers* cannot go without the *senders'* financial support:

Romans 10:14-15:

> 14   **How then shall they call on Him in whom they have not believed? And how shall they believe in Him of whom they have not heard? And how shall they hear without a preacher?**

> 15   **And how shall they preach unless they are sent? As it is written: "How beautiful are the feet of those who preach the gospel of peace, who bring glad tidings of good things!"**

Look at Verse 17:

The Purpose of Prosperity

So then faith comes by hearing, and hearing by the word of God.

The unsaved world needs preachers to come and minister the Word of Salvation so they can get saved and learn how to live victoriously in Christ. When we think of preachers, we think of pastors. The word *preacher* doesn't necessarily limit itself to "pastor, evangelist, prophet or a teacher." The word *preacher* literally means "proclaimer" — a verbalizer of the gospel. Any Christian can share the gospel anywhere. You don't have to stand in a pulpit to do that. Someone has to speak the Word of God, because faith comes by hearing and that is how people are going to get saved.

By participating in and supporting various media, such as radio and television, we can all be either *goers* or *senders*. Now, of course, we have the Internet, which has become a major avenue for spreading the gospel. There are CD's, videotapes and audiotapes, which are important ways of sharing God's Word. God created all these things for the proclamation of the gospel. But the Church is so antiquated in its thinking that it sits on its backside and lets the world pirate all of God's ideas, and then the world takes those ideas and makes millions from the gadgets so that folk can go to hell with them.

Where do you think the world gets the ideas for all these mechanical things? It is marvelous what man can do with electronics these days. That knowledge comes from God, not the devil. The devil is not a creator; he has never created anything. He only takes advantage of what God has already created, and then he misconstrues and distorts it.

130

Benefiting From Our Partnership With God

Once you give or plant your seed, you need to understand how to receive from your giving because it is not automatic. As I said before, you have an enemy who will be out there trying to steal what belongs to you. It is important to stand by faith when you are claiming your return, and not be deterred in your stand. You cannot be double-minded and start doubting when you do not see results right away. Your steadfastness will produce what God promised.

James 1:5-8:

5   If any of you lacks wisdom, let him ask of God, who gives to all liberally and without reproach, and it will be given to him.

6   But let him ask in faith, with no doubting, for he who doubts is like a wave of the sea driven and tossed by the wind.

7   For let not that man suppose that he will receive anything from the Lord;

8   *he is* a double-minded man, unstable in all his ways.

It is amazing to me that even though we are reading information from the Bible that is about 2,000 years old, the game plan is still the same. We still have folk today who are

131

double-minded, inconsistent and unable to be counted on. If you want to receive the blessings that God says are yours when you bring in the tithes and offerings, you need to stand by faith and lay hold of your return, and not give up no matter how things may look in the natural. That is what I had to do, and I am living proof that it works. It is your stand of faith that will open up the floodgates on your behalf.

If you have been a wise steward, you should get to the point where you have a surplus of funds, and where you don't have to believe God for every single thing you need. Every time you need a pair of shoes, you should not have to exercise your faith for them. Every time you have to pay a bill, you should not have to believe God for the money. You want to get past that.

It has been years since I have had to use my faith to believe for anything. God has already provided for me and my family's needs. But when I did have to use my faith, I had to be sure that wherever I gave I would get a return. It is actually like investing. I cannot go out and plant my seed on a blacktop parking lot because it is not going to give me a harvest, and I would be out of business if I continued to do that.

You have to be wise enough to be able to discern where you are supposed to sow your seed in order to get a continuous return on what you sow. It is a reciprocal transaction: You plant seed, get a return; plant seed, get a return; plant seed, get a return. And your return should continue to increase until you get to a place where you have a surplus.

Years ago, I had to believe for everything. I had to believe God even for a pencil one time. You may think I am joking, but I had to believe for everything we needed because that was where we were. By using our faith and following God's plan for prosperity, we now have a large surplus. We learned long ago not to eat up our seed. We could go out and buy another car, but why should we? We have enough cars, and all are in good condition. We would much rather plant seed into the spreading of the gospel so that the lost can be saved.

I want to discuss in more detail principles in reference to investing in the gospel that you can put into operation to become a channel of blessing and a worker together with God. In order to do this, you have to get out of the box society has you in so you can be your own person, one to whom God can afford to pipe wealth.

Some believers are bound by the system. God cannot afford to give them a lot of money at one time because they would squander it, just as they have squandered what they have now. For Him to seek and save the lost, He has to be able to pipe the wealth to people He can count on to do as He wants. I covered these scriptures earlier, but they are so apropos here that I want to cover them again:

James 1:5:

If any of you lacks wisdom, let him ask of God, who gives to all liberally and without reproach, and it will be given to him.

When you are in a bad situation and you do not know what to do, the first thing you want to do is what James says: Ask God. But I will tell you this, getting out of your financial dilemma is first and foremost a heart decision. If you do not have the resolve to get out, the system will keep you bound and will always show you some apparent legitimate reason why you need to stay that way. There has to be a resolve, and there has to be a willingness to pay the price to be financially free. If you are bound, you are paying a price one way or another.

When my wife and I decided to get out of the financial bind we were in, we made a pact between the two of us that we would not buy anything we did not absolutely need; we would not buy anything on time or use a credit card except in a life-or-death situation. Self-denial is painful. Your body and mind will fight you every step of the way, but you have to fight to keep your resolve. You have to rise above that pain for the purpose of getting to your wealthy place.

So we stopped buying. We did not even buy a Christmas tree for a couple of years or even gifts for the children. You have to do whatever you have to do to get where you want to be.

If any of you lacks wisdom, ask God to give you the wisdom to help you get out of debt. Don't be hardheaded; it doesn't diminish your manhood to say you blew it. Obviously, you lacked wisdom or you would not have gotten into a financial bind in the first place if you had exercised wisdom instead of over-extending yourself with those credit cards. The real man or woman is the one who is willing to admit that he or she made a mistake and wants to correct the mistake. The fool is the one who keeps doing the same dumb thing.

James 1:6-8:

> **6** **But let him ask in faith** [not in fear], **with no doubting** [you cannot doubt],

> **for he who doubts is like a wave of the sea driven and tossed by the wind.**
>
> 7   **For let not that man supposed that he will receive anything from the Lord;**
>
> 8   **he is a double-minded man, unstable in all his ways.**

You have to ask in faith, with no doubting that God will give you the wisdom. He gave Betty and me the wisdom and showed me how to get out of the mess we were in. In fact, we were so messed up, that Betty said to me at one point, after I told her that I was doing the best I could: *"Your best is just not good enough."*

People play the lottery thinking they can get out of their financial dilemma that way. They are living in a fool's dream. People who play the lottery are people who are out of control. *"Yes, but, Pastor, I will tithe to the church."* Sure you will. You will not give God anything because you have not given Him anything before, and that is why you are in the situation you are in. God does not rely on any Lotto to get money to you. His method is sowing and reaping, and paying tithes and giving offerings. If you do that, the Lord will bless you, and cause you to be a blessing to others.

The Prayer of Agreement

One of the best ways for a married couple to solve their situation is to come into agreement to get out of debt:

135

Matthew 18:19:

"Again I say to you that if two of you agree on earth concerning anything that they ask, it will be done for them by My Father in heaven."

The husband and wife have to be in agreement. They cannot go in different directions or the prayer of agreement, according to the above scripture, will not work. If the couple cannot be in agreement with each other, they have no business being married to each other, because there will constantly be challenges in the marriage.

Now let me clear that up, because that is just what some Christians want to hear. I didn't mean they should go out and get a divorce because they cannot agree on certain issues. That would not be pleasing to God either. What I mean is if a couple loves each other, why can't they be in agreement? What they need to do is to negotiate until they come to a place where they can agree. We all have our own opinions, and that is not bad in and of itself. But a married couple should be able to come to agreement on some things, and getting out of debt definitely should be one of the things they agree on.

Often what couples do is magnify what they do not agree on and waste a lot of time fussing, fighting and arguing about that, not realizing that if they would agree, they would be absolutely amazed how their agreement could turn things around. Then when they plant their seed and agree for the return, and the return keeps coming back, they will have more seed to plant in the future, and debt can be for them a thing of the past. This is where their faith comes in: Following God's plan and believing that what He says will happen, will happen.

The Prayer of Faith

Mark 11:24:

"Therefore I say to you, whatever things you ask when you pray, believe that you receive them, and you will have them."

When you plant your seed by investing in the proclamation of the gospel, you should claim the return on your giving and confess: *"Father, we thank you. We believe we receive our return."* This is a faith principle that works for claiming the desires of your heart, as well. You lay claim to your desires by faith, and then you believe God that you have them and continue to make a daily confession, *"I believe that I have my desire; I believe that I have received, and I thank You Father."*

In fact, I do this in my daily prayer time in reference to all the issues of my life, and I have been doing this for 30 years. I am telling you this so that you can get into the flow. But in actuality, I don't lay claim to any needs anymore, because I have the system going so well that it has become basically a maintenance system for me. The last time we actually laid claim to something was many years ago when my wife and I came into agreement to pay off our house. Our confession of faith that it was paid off manifested almost thirteen years later. The Word of God works, and if you will work it, it will work for you.

The final thing is to praise God for the return, and you praise Him for the answer or return before you ever experience it. That is called walking by faith and not by sight. The way sight comes is by operating in faith. So when you pray and lay claim to the things that are yours based on the Word, you can expect to prosper.

God wants His children to prosper. He wants to pipe the wealth to us so that through us and with us, He can seek and save that which was lost. The overflow will meet our own needs, as well as give us the desires of our hearts. That is God's covenant of wealth and the purpose of prosperity.

About the Author

Dr. Frederick K.C. Price is the founder and pastor of Crenshaw Christian Center in Los Angeles, California. He is known worldwide as a teacher of the biblical principles of faith, healing, prosperity and the Holy Spirit. During his more than 47 years in ministry, countless lives have been changed by his dynamic and insightful teachings that truly "tell it like it is."

His television program, *Ever Increasing Faith*, has been broadcast throughout the world for more than 20 years and airs in 15 of the 20 largest markets in America, reaching an audience of more than 15 million households each week. His radio program is heard on stations across the world, including the continent of Europe via short-wave radio. He is the author of more than 50 popular books teaching practical application of biblical principles.

Dr. Price pastors one of America's largest church congregations, with a membership of 20 thousand. The church sanctuary, the FaithDome, is among the most notable and largest in the nation, with seating capacity of more than 10 thousand.

In 1990, Dr. Price founded the Fellowship of Inner City Word of Faith Ministries (FICWFM). Members of FICWFM include more than 300 churches from all over the United States and various countries. The Fellowship, which meets regionally throughout the year and hosts an annual convention, is not a denomination. Its mission is to provide fellowship, leadership, guidance and a spiritual covering for those desiring a standard of excellence in ministry. Members share methods and experiences commonly faced by ministries in the inner cities. Their focus is how to apply the Word of Faith to solve their challenges.

Dr. Price holds an honorary Doctorate of Divinity degree from Oral Roberts University and an honorary diploma from Rhema Bible Training Center.

On September 6, 2000, Dr. Price was the first black pastor to speak at Town Hall Los Angeles. In 1998, he was the recipient of two prestigious awards: The Horatio Alger Award, which is given each year. This prestigious honor is bestowed upon ten "outstanding Americans who exemplify inspirational success, triumph over adversity, and an uncommon commitment to helping others …." He also received the 1998 Southern Christian Leadership Conference's Kelly Miller Smith Interfaith Award. This award is given to clergy who have made the most significant contribution through religious expression affecting the nation and the world.

Books by
Frederick K.C. Price, D.D.

INTEGRITY
The Guarantee of Success

HIGHER FINANCE
How to Live Debt-Free

RACE, RELIGION & RACISM, VOLUME 1
A Bold Encounter With Division in the Church

RACE, RELIGION & RACISM, VOLUME 2
Perverting the Gospel to Subjugate a People

RACE, RELIGION & RACISM, VOLUME 3
Jesus, Christianity and Islam

THE TRUTH ABOUT ... THE BIBLE

THE TRUTH ABOUT ... DEATH

THE TRUTH ABOUT ... DISASTERS

THE TRUTH ABOUT ... FATE

THE TRUTH ABOUT ... FEAR

THE TRUTH ABOUT ... HOMOSEXUALITY

THE TRUTH ABOUT ... RACE

THE TRUTH ABOUT ... WORRY

THE TRUTH ABOUT ... GIVING

LIVING IN HOSTILE TERRITORY
A Survival Guide for the Overcoming Christian

141

The Purpose of Prosperity

DR. PRICE'S GOLDEN NUGGETS
A Treasury of Wisdom for Both Ministers and Laypeople

BUILDING ON A FIRM FOUNDATION

FIVE LITTLE FOXES OF FAITH

THE HOLY SPIRIT:
The Helper We All Need

THE CHRISTIAN FAMILY:
Practical Insight for Family Living

IDENTIFIED WITH CHRIST:
A Complete Cycle From Defeat to Victory

THE CHASTENING OF THE LORD

TESTING THE SPIRITS

BEWARE! THE LIES OF SATAN

THE WAY, THE WALK,
AND THE WARFARE OF THE BELIEVER
(A Verse-by-Verse Study on the Book of Ephesians)

THREE KEYS TO POSITIVE CONFESSION

THE PROMISED LAND
(A New Era for the Body of Christ)

A NEW LAW FOR A NEW PEOPLE

THE VICTORIOUS, OVERCOMING LIFE
(A Verse-by-Verse Study on the Book of Colossians)

NAME IT AND CLAIM IT!
The Power of Positive Confession

Books by Frederick K.C. Price, D.D.

*PRACTICAL SUGGESTIONS FOR
SUCCESSFUL MINISTRY*

WALKING IN GOD'S WORD
Through His Promises

HOMOSEXUALITY:
State of Birth or State of Mind?

CONCERNING THOSE WHO HAVE FALLEN ASLEEP

THE ORIGIN OF SATAN

LIVING IN THE REALM OF THE SPIRIT

HOW TO BELIEVE GOD FOR A MATE

THANK GOD FOR EVERYTHING?

FAITH, FOOLISHNESS, OR PRESUMPTION?

THE HOLY SPIRIT —
The Missing Ingredient

NOW FAITH IS

HOW TO OBTAIN STRONG FAITH
Six Principles

IS HEALING FOR ALL?

HOW FAITH WORKS

FAITH'S GREATEST ENEMIES